Cadbury

mini eggs

COOKBOOK

Cadbury

mini eggs

COOKBOOK

60 CRACKING CADBURY MINI EGGS RECIPES

HarperCollins*Publishers*

HarperCollins*Publishers*
1 London Bridge Street
London SE1 9GF
www.harpercollins.co.uk

HarperCollins*Publishers*
1st Floor, Watermarque Building
Ringsend Road,
Dublin 4, Ireland

First published by HarperCollins*Publishers* 2021

10 9 8 7 6 5 4 3 2

© Mondelez Europe GmbH 2021

The author asserts the moral right to be
identified as the author of this work

CADBURY and MINI EGGS are registered
trademarks of Cadbury UK Limited, used
under licence

Recipes created by Heather Thomas
Photography by Steve Lee
Food styling by Jayne Cross
Prop styling by Rebecca Newport

A catalogue record of this book is available
from the British Library

ISBN 978-0-00-843418-2

Printed and bound in Latvia

MIX
Paper from
responsible sources
FSC™ C007454

FSC
www.fsc.org

This book is produced from independently certified FSC™ paper
to ensure responsible forest management.

For more information visit: www.harpercollins.co.uk/green

A SERVING OF THE RECIPES
IN THIS BOOK SHOULD BE SEEN
AS AN INDULGENT TREAT, BEST
ENJOYED ONLY OCCASIONALLY.
IT IS IMPORTANT TO FOLLOW
A HEALTHY BALANCED DIET
AND ACTIVE LIFESTYLE.

NONE OF THESE RECIPES ARE
SUITABLE FOR MILK OR DAIRY
ALLERGY SUFFERERS. IF YOU
DO SUFFER WITH AN ALLERGY,
PLEASE CHECK THE INGREDIENTS
LIST ON EACH RECIPE.

WARNING: CHOKING HAZARD.
CADBURY MINI EGGS ARE NOT
SUITABLE FOR CHILDREN
UNDER FOUR.

CONTENTS

INTRODUCTION

OUR EGGS MAY BE MINI, BUT OUR IMAGINATION IS MIGHTY – AND THERE'S NOTHING SMALL ABOUT THE WIDE RANGE OF RECIPES HERE.

Packed with 60 yummy new recipes that showcase the goodness of Mini Eggs, this cookbook offers lots of tasty treats that are fun to make and even more scrummy to eat!

There are recipes for sweet things ranging from baked Alaska to waffles and from meringues to muffins, so what are you waiting for? Let's get messy in the kitchen and give your favourite bakes a tasty Mini Eggs twist.

FIND CHOCOLATE FUDGE
BROWNIE BITES ON PAGE 38

TURN TO PAGE 10
FOR ROCKY ROAD

TRAY BAKES
& CAKES

MINI EGGS ROCKY ROAD

Enjoy the bumps of Mini Eggs in these rocky road bakes when you bite into the delectable mixture of chewy marshmallow and buttery biscuit.

MAKES 24
PREP TIME 15 MINS
CHILLING TIME
2–3 HOURS

400g Cadbury Dairy Milk chocolate, broken into squares
150g digestive biscuits
50g mini marshmallows
90g Cadbury Mini Eggs

1. Line a 30 x 20cm baking tin with baking parchment.
2. Put the chocolate squares into a large glass bowl and microwave them for 20–30 seconds. Take out the bowl and stir the chocolate, then repeat until it is all melted. Alternatively, place the bowl over a pan of gently simmering water until the chocolate has melted.
3. Put the digestive biscuits into a sealable plastic bag and bash them with a rolling pin until you have a mixture of different-sized pieces. You want some quite big crunchy pieces – not just crumbs.
4. Stir the crushed biscuits and marshmallows into the melted chocolate until everything is well combined and coated.
5. Transfer the mixture to the lined tin, pushing it into the corners and levelling the top. Push in the Cadbury Mini Eggs, distributing them evenly, and press them down with a spatula or the back of a spoon.
6. Chill the mixture in the fridge for 2–3 hours (or overnight) until it is set. Cut it into 24 squares and store them in an airtight container in the fridge for up to 2 weeks.

PER SERVING

| 143 kcals | 7g fat | 4g sat fat |
| 14g sugar | 0.08g salt | |

MINI EGGS BUTTERFLY SURPRISE CAKES

Like a butterfly emerging from a cocoon, these cupcakes contain their own surprise! So why not try making this Mini Eggs twist on a classic?

MAKES 12
PREP TIME 20 MINS
COOKING TIME
15–20 MINS

100g low-fat spread
100g soft brown sugar
2 medium free-range eggs, beaten
75g self-raising flour
½ tsp baking powder
25g cocoa powder
1 tbsp skimmed milk
12 Cadbury Mini Eggs

FOR THE CHOCOLATE BUTTERCREAM
50g butter, softened
75g icing sugar, plus extra for dusting
1 tbsp cocoa powder
a few drops of vanilla extract
1 tsp skimmed milk

You will need a piping bag with a star-shaped nozzle

1. Preheat the oven to 180°C/160°C fan/gas mark 4. Place 12 paper muffin cases in a 12-hole muffin tin.
2. Beat the spread and sugar together using an electric hand mixer or a food mixer until they are light and fluffy. Beat in the beaten egg a bit at a time.
3. Sift the flour, baking powder and cocoa powder into the bowl and fold them in gently. Slacken the mixture with the milk.
4. Divide the mixture between the paper cases and bake the cakes in the preheated oven for 15–20 minutes until they are well risen and a thin skewer inserted into a cake comes out clean. Cool them on a wire rack.
5. Cut a shallow cone-shaped piece out of the centre of each cake and place a Mini Egg in the hollow. Set aside the cones.
6. To make the chocolate buttercream beat the butter and icing sugar until they are soft and creamy. Beat in the cocoa powder, vanilla extract and milk.
7. Spoon the mixture into a piping bag with a star-shaped nozzle and pipe a rosette on top of each cupcake to cover the Mini Egg. Cut each cone in half to form wings and place these on top of the cakes. Dust them lightly with icing sugar and serve. The cakes will keep well in an airtight container in a cool place for 3–4 days.

PER SERVING

177 kcals	9g fat	4.1g sat fat
17g sugar	0.3g salt	

MINI EGGS SKINNY BROWNIES

These skinny brownies are a gooey treat packed with the crunch that only Mini Eggs can bring.

MAKES 9
PREP TIME 20 MINS
COOKING TIME 25–30 MINS

125g reduced-fat sunflower spread, plus extra for greasing
125g dark molasses or soft brown sugar
2 medium free-range eggs
125g self-raising flour
50g cocoa powder
½ tsp baking powder
125g 0% fat Greek yoghurt
2 tbsp skimmed milk
1 tsp vanilla extract
60g Cadbury Mini Eggs

1. Preheat the oven to 180°C/160°C fan/gas mark 4. Grease a 20cm square cake tin and line with baking parchment.
2. Beat the sunflower spread and sugar together in a food mixer or with a hand-held electric whisk, until they are light and fluffy.
3. Beat in the eggs one at a time and then sift in the flour, cocoa powder and baking powder. Beat well and then whisk in the yoghurt, milk and vanilla extract. The mixture should be smooth but not too stiff – add a little more milk to slacken it if necessary.
4. Put half the Cadbury Mini Eggs into a sealable plastic bag and smash them into small pieces with a rolling pin or meat mallet. Alternatively, crush them in a pestle and mortar. Fold them into the cake mixture and pour it into the prepared tin. Level the top.
5. Crush the remaining Cadbury Mini Eggs into large pieces in the same way. Sprinkle them over the mixture. Bake the brownie in the preheated oven for 25–30 minutes until it is cooked and well risen.
6. Leave the brownie to cool in the tin and then cut into 9 squares. Store them in an airtight container in the fridge and eat within 4–5 days.

PER SERVING

206 kcals	7.5g fat	2.6g sat fat
14g sugar		0.3g salt

MINI TIP

TO TEST WHETHER THE BROWNIE IS COOKED, INSERT A THIN SKEWER INTO THE CENTRE – IT SHOULD COME OUT CLEAN.

MINI EGGS CHOC CHIP ROCK CAKES

Mini Eggs choc chip rock cakes that aren't tough to crack. Perfect for dunking into a glass of milk or hot chocolate.

MAKES 16
PREP TIME 15 MINS
COOKING TIME 15 MINS

250g self-raising flour
2 tsp baking powder
125g butter, cut into small pieces
60g Cadbury Mini Eggs
60g soft brown sugar
50g Cadbury Bournville chocolate, chopped into pieces
1 large free-range egg, beaten
3 tbsp skimmed milk

1. Preheat the oven to 200°C/180°C fan/gas mark 6. Lightly butter 2 baking trays.
2. Sift the flour and baking powder into a large mixing bowl and rub in the butter with your fingertips until the mixture resembles light breadcrumbs.
3. Put the Cadbury Mini Eggs into a sealable plastic bag and smash them into small to medium pieces with a rolling pin or meat mallet. Alternatively, crush them in a pestle and mortar.
4. Add the pieces to the flour and butter mixture in the bowl along with the sugar and chocolate. Mix in the beaten egg and milk to form a slightly sticky dough. If it's too dry, add a little more milk.
5. Drop 16 spoonfuls of the dough on to the prepared baking trays. Bake in the preheated oven for about 15 minutes until the rock cakes are well risen and golden brown.
6. Remove the cakes from the baking tray and cool them on a wire rack before storing them in an airtight container for up to 2–3 days.

PER SERVING

176 kcals	9.8g fat	2.8g sat fat
8g sugar	0.06g salt	

MINI EGGS
PEANUT BUTTER CUPS

These indulgent cups showcase the moreish flavour of peanut butter along with the crunchy bite of Mini Eggs. They will be enjoyed by kids and adults alike. This recipe is a very tasty but indulgent treat, best enjoyed on special occasions.

MAKES 12
PREP TIME 20 MINS
COOKING TIME 6–8 MINS
FREEZING TIME 45–60 MINS

300g Cadbury Bournville chocolate, broken into squares
12 Cadbury Mini Eggs
50g icing sugar
25g butter, at room temperature
125g smooth peanut butter
300g Cadbury Dairy Milk chocolate, broken into squares

PER SERVING

277 kcals	16.5g fat	8g sat fat
25.8g sugar	0.01g salt	

1. Line two muffin tins with 12 paper or foil cases.
2. Melt the Cadbury Bournville chocolate in a microwave or a heatproof bowl set over a pan of simmering water. Divide the melted chocolate between the 12 paper or foil cases to cover the bases evenly. Place a Mini Egg in the centre of each one and put the muffin tins in the freezer for 15–20 minutes until the chocolate sets hard.
3. While the chocolate is freezing, put the icing sugar, butter and peanut butter in a bowl and beat them with a food mixer or a hand-held electric whisk until they are creamy and smooth.
4. Remove the muffin tins from the freezer and divide the peanut butter mixture between the cases, making sure that the Cadbury Mini Eggs are covered. Gently smooth and level the tops. Return the tins to the freezer for 15–20 minutes.
5. Melt the Cadbury Dairy Milk chocolate in a microwave or a heatproof bowl over a pan of simmering water. Spoon the melted chocolate over the top of the peanut butter mixture in a single layer to cover it evenly. Return the tins to the freezer for 15–20 minutes until the chocolate is set.
6. You can keep the peanut butter cups in a container in the fridge for up to a week. Serve them chilled or at room temperature.

MINI EGGS CRUMB FUDGE SQUARES

Gooey squares that are the perfect combination of creamy fudge and crunchy Mini Eggs. This recipe is a very tasty but indulgent treat, best enjoyed on special occasions.

MAKES 16
PREP TIME 15–20 MINS
CHILLING TIME 2–3 HOURS

100g butter
1 tbsp caster sugar
1 tbsp golden syrup
2 tbsp cocoa powder
150g reduced-fat ginger biscuits
90g Cadbury Mini Eggs
125g Cadbury Bournville chocolate, broken into squares

PER SERVING

164 kcals | 8.7g fat | 5.6g sat fat
11.7g sugar | 0.08g salt

1. Line a 20 x 20cm baking tin with baking parchment.
2. Melt the butter in a saucepan set over a low heat. Stir in the sugar, golden syrup and cocoa powder, then remove the pan from the heat.
3. Crush the biscuits by putting them in a sealable plastic bag and bashing them into small pieces and crumbs with a rolling pin. Stir the pieces into the chocolate mixture.
4. Crush two-thirds of the Cadbury Mini Eggs in the same way and add them to the mixture. Mix well, making sure that everything is well coated.
5. Press the mixture into the lined tin and spread it out evenly, levelling the top with the back of a spatula or a wooden spoon.
6. Put the remaining Cadbury Mini Eggs in a glass bowl with the chocolate squares and put the bowl in the microwave for 20–30 seconds. Take out the bowl and press the eggs with the back of a spoon to break them up. Repeat until the chocolate has all melted. Alternatively, place the bowl over a pan of gently simmering water until the chocolate has melted.
7. Spread the melted chocolate over the crumb fudge mixture and chill it in the fridge for 2–3 hours until it is firm and the chocolate topping is set. Cut it into 16 squares and store them in an airtight container in the fridge to keep as solid as possible for up to 2 weeks.

MINI EGGS SPRINGTIME CAKE

The lively lemon flavour of this cake along with the thyme and lavender decorations combine to make a delectable treat that reflects the freshness of spring.

SERVES 14
PREP TIME 20 MINS
COOKING TIME 40–45 MINS

200g runny thyme honey (or other runny honey)
4 medium free-range eggs
75ml light olive oil
grated zest and juice of 1 lemon
2 tsp fresh thyme leaves
1 tsp edible dried lavender (optional)
200g plain flour
1 tsp baking powder
100g ground almonds
14 Cadbury Mini Eggs
flowering sprigs of fresh thyme and lavender, to decorate (optional)

FOR THE LEMON ICING
100g icing sugar
grated zest of 1 lemon
1–2 tbsp lemon juice

1. Preheat the oven to 160°C/140°C fan/gas mark 3. Lightly oil a 23cm cake tin and line it with baking parchment.
2. Using a food mixer or a hand-held electric whisk, beat the honey and eggs until they are well blended. Beat in the olive oil, lemon zest and juice together with the thyme and the dried lavender, if using.
3. Sift in the flour and baking powder and beat the mixture well. Add the ground almonds and beat again until everything is well combined and you have a smooth mixture. If it's too thick you can slacken it with a little milk or some more lemon juice.
4. Spoon the mixture into the lined cake tin and bake it in the preheated oven for 40–45 minutes until the cake is well risen and golden brown. Test whether it's cooked by inserting a thin skewer into the middle. If it comes out clean, remove the cake from the oven and leave it to cool.
5. To make the lemon icing sift the icing sugar into a bowl and stir in the lemon zest and juice.
6. Remove the cake from the tin and drizzle the icing over the top. Place the Cadbury Mini Eggs at regular intervals around the top of the cake. Just before serving arrange some flowering sprigs of lavender and thyme in the centre. Store the cake in an airtight container. It will last well for up to 5 days. Remove the herb sprigs before storing.

PER SERVING

247 kcals	11g fat	1.9g sat fat
19.8g sugar	0.1g salt	

MINI TIP

INSTEAD OF FRESH THYME, TRY USING ROSEMARY OR EVEN TARRAGON.

MINI EGGS SKINNY CARROT CAKE

There's no guarantee that this creamy cake will help you see in the dark, but it's so delicious that you'll certainly come back for more.

MAKES 16
PREP TIME 20 MINS
COOKING TIME 45 MINS

175g soft light brown sugar
120ml sunflower oil
3 medium free-range eggs, beaten
225g carrots, grated
grated zest and juice of
  1 orange
175g wholemeal self-raising flour
1 tsp baking powder
1 tsp ground cinnamon
½ tsp grated nutmeg

FOR THE CREAMY FROSTING
100g extra-light soft cheese
75g thick 0% fat Greek yoghurt
1 tbsp icing sugar
grated zest of 1 orange
16 Cadbury Mini Eggs

1. Preheat the oven to 180°C/160°C fan/gas mark 4. Lightly oil a 20cm square cake tin and line it with baking parchment.

2. In a food mixer or food processor, beat together the sugar, oil and eggs until they are well blended. (Alternatively, beat them in a large mixing bowl with an electric hand mixer.) Beat in the grated carrot and the orange zest and juice.
   Then sift in the flour, baking powder and spices and mix everything together thoroughly.

3. Pour the cake mixture into the lined cake tin and smooth the top. Bake the cake in the preheated oven for 45 minutes, or until it is well risen and a skewer inserted into the centre comes out clean. Leave it to cool in the tin.

4. To make the creamy frosting put the soft cheese, yoghurt, icing sugar and orange zest in a bowl and mix until they are well blended and smooth.

5. Spread the frosting over the cake and cut it into 16 squares. Place a Mini Egg on each square. Store the cake in a sealed container in the fridge for 3–4 days.

PER SERVING

192 kcals	9.3g fat	1.9g sat fat
15g sugar	0.1g salt	

MINI EGGS CHOCOLATE AND RASPBERRY ROULADE

We've made the roulade even more innovative with our not-so-secret special Mini Eggs ingredient. Fruity, crunchy, creamy *and* chocolatey! The flavour of this raspberry roulade will have your friends and family rolling over for more.

SERVES 8
PREP TIME 25 MINS
COOKING TIME 7-9 MINS

1 tsp sunflower oil
3 medium free-range eggs
60g caster sugar
70g plain flour
3 tbsp cocoa powder

FOR THE RASPBERRY FILLING
30g Cadbury Mini Eggs
175g extra-light soft cheese
100g low-fat raspberry yoghurt
100g fresh raspberries
1 tbsp icing sugar, for dusting

You will need a 28 x 18cm Swiss roll tin

PER SERVING

174 kcals	6.5g fat	2.8g sat fat
12g sugar		0.3g salt

1. Preheat the oven to 220°C/200°C fan/gas mark 7. Lightly brush a 28 x 18cm Swiss roll tin with half the oil. Line it with baking parchment and brush it with the remaining oil.

2. Using an electric hand mixer or food mixer, whisk together the eggs and sugar for about 5 minutes until you have a very light and pale mixture.

3. Sift the flour and cocoa powder into the mixture and fold them in gently with a metal spoon in a figure-of-eight movement, until everything is thoroughly mixed and a uniform colour.

4. Pour the mixture into the lined tin and spread it out gently with a palette knife to cover the whole area evenly.

5. Bake the cake in the preheated oven for 7–9 minutes until it is risen and firm and springs back when you press it lightly with a finger. Remove it by turning the tin upside down over a large sheet of baking parchment. Peel away the lining paper and trim the edges of the cake with a sharp knife. Cover it with a damp tea towel and set it aside to cool.

6. To make the filling put the Cadbury Mini Eggs into a sealable plastic bag and smash them into small to medium pieces with a rolling pin or meat mallet.

7. In a bowl, mix together the soft cheese and yoghurt. Stir in the raspberries and crushed Cadbury Mini Eggs. Spread the mixture over the cold cake and then roll it up from one short end.

8. Place the roulade on a serving plate with the join underneath, and dust it lightly with icing sugar. Cut it into slices to serve. You can store it in a sealed container in the fridge for up to 24 hours.

MINI EGGS
BLONDIES

These chewy blondies are a treat for white chocolate fans. Enjoy the creaminess of the chocolate combined with the crunchy bite of the crushed Mini Eggs.

MAKES 16
PREP TIME 20 MINS
COOKING TIME 20–25 MINS
CHILLING TIME 15–30 MINS

100g butter
125g soft light brown sugar
2 medium free-range eggs
1 tsp vanilla extract
125g self-raising flour
75g Cadbury White Chocolate Buttons
30g Cadbury Mini Eggs

1. Preheat the oven to 190°C/170°C fan/gas mark 5. Lightly grease a 20 x 20cm cake tin and line it with baking parchment.
2. Put the butter in a saucepan set over a low heat and when it melts stir in the sugar. Turn up the heat a little and when the mixture starts to colour and turn golden, remove the pan from the heat.
3. Whisk the eggs and vanilla extract in a large bowl and then beat in the butter and sugar mixture. Add the flour and fold it in gently with a metal spoon until the mixture is well combined and smooth. Pour it into the lined cake tin.
4. Bake the blondie in the preheated oven for 20–25 minutes until it is well risen and golden and a skewer inserted into the centre comes out clean. Leave it to cool in the tin and then cut it into 16 squares.

MINI TIP

TO ADD CRUNCH, GENTLY FOLD IN 50g CHOPPED PECANS BEFORE POURING THE CAKE MIXTURE INTO THE TIN.

PER SERVING

133 kcals	7g fat	4g sat fat
10g sugar		0.1g salt

5. Put the Cadbury White Chocolate Buttons in a large glass bowl in the microwave for 20–30 seconds. Take out the bowl and stir the chocolate, then repeat until it is all melted. Alternatively, place the bowl over a pan of gently simmering water and stir until the buttons have melted.

6. Crush the Cadbury Mini Eggs into small pieces by placing them in a sealable plastic bag and smashing them with a rolling pin or meat mallet. Alternatively, use a pestle and mortar. Spread out the pieces on a plate.

7. Take a blondie square and spread the melted chocolate over half of it. Place it on a baking sheet lined with baking parchment and sprinkle some crushed Mini Eggs pieces over the top, pressing them lightly into the melted chocolate. Repeat with all the remaining blondies.

8. Chill the blondies in the fridge for 15–30 minutes until the chocolate is set. Store the Blondies in an airtight container for up to 3 days (or for 5–6 days if stored in the fridge).

MINI EGGS CHOCOLATE SIMNEL CAKE

This classic cake makes a beautiful centrepiece for Easter celebrations. The pastel colours of the Mini Eggs together with the yellow marzipan perfectly reflect the colours of springtime. This recipe is a very tasty but indulgent treat, best enjoyed on special occasions.

SERVES 14
PREP TIME 25 MINS
COOKING TIME 1 HOUR

200g butter, softened
200g soft dark brown sugar
4 medium free-range eggs
200g plain flour
1 tsp baking powder
75g cocoa powder
grated zest and juice of 1 orange
200g marzipan
14 Cadbury Mini Eggs
spring flowers to decorate, e.g. pansies, freesias, violets (optional)

PER SERVING

| 327 kcals | 17g fat | 8.9g sat fat |
| 25.7g sugar | | 0.1g salt |

1. Preheat the oven to 160°C/140°C fan/gas mark 3. Grease a 20cm round cake tin and line it with baking parchment.
2. Beat the butter and sugar until they are light and creamy with an electric hand mixer or in a food mixer.
3. Beat in the eggs one at a time, adding a sprinkling of flour to stop the mixture curdling. Sift in the flour, baking powder and cocoa powder and mix them in gently until everything is well combined. Add the orange zest and juice and mix well. If the mixture is very thick, you can slacken it with a little milk.
4. Transfer the mixture to the lined cake tin and bake it in the preheated oven for 1 hour, or until it is well risen and coming away from the sides of the tin. Insert a thin skewer into the centre – if it comes out clean, it's cooked. Leave the cake to cool in the tin before turning it out.
5. Roll out the marzipan into a 20cm circle, then carefully lift it with the rolling pin and place it on top of the cold cake.
6. Place the Cadbury Mini Eggs around the edge of the cake, pressing them lightly into the marzipan. Just before serving, arrange a few spring flowers in the centre. Store the cake in an airtight container for up to 4–5 days.

MINI EGGS BUNNY CUPCAKES

Our moist and crunchy Mini Eggs bunny cupcakes are a scrummy treat, and will look gorgeous at an Easter party or egg hunt. This recipe is a very tasty but indulgent treat, best enjoyed on special occasions.

MAKES 16
PREP TIME 30 MINS
COOKING TIME
15–20 MINS

200g butter, softened
200g caster sugar
3 medium free-range eggs
200g self-raising flour
50g cocoa powder
150g natural low-fat yoghurt
16 Cadbury Mini Eggs
200g ready-made white fondant icing
brown food colouring

FOR THE BUTTERCREAM
75g butter, softened
150g icing sugar
green food colouring
40g desiccated coconut

PER SERVING

367 kcals	18.8g fat	11.6g sat fat
34g sugar		0.1g salt

1. Preheat the oven to 180°C/160°C fan/gas mark 4. Place 16 paper muffin cases in 2 muffin tins.

2. Using an electric hand mixer or a food mixer, beat the butter and sugar together until they are light and fluffy. Beat in the eggs one at a time and then sift in the flour and cocoa powder and mix in gently. Add the yoghurt and mix until everything is smooth and combined.

3. Divide the mixture between the paper cases and bake the cakes in the preheated oven for 15–20 minutes until they are well risen and a thin skewer inserted into a cake comes out clean. Cool them on a wire rack.

4. Cut a shallow cone-shaped piece out of the centre of each cake and place a Mini Egg in the hollow. Trim the pointed ends of the cones and use them to cover each Mini Egg.

5. To make the buttercream beat the butter and sugar in a bowl until smooth. Add a few drops of green food colouring and mix well. Spread the mixture over the cupcakes to cover the tops.

6. Place the coconut in a small sealable bag with 2–3 drops of green food colouring and shake well until the coconut is evenly coloured. Sprinkle it over the buttercream to resemble grass.

7. Add a few drops of brown food colouring to two-thirds of the fondant icing and roll into 16 balls to make the rabbits' bodies.

8. Halve the remaining white icing. From one half make 16 small balls for the tails and 32 tiny balls for the feet from the other half. Use a little cooled boiled water to stick on the tails and feet – flatten the feet slightly to look like they are tucked under the body.

9. Place a bunny in the centre of each cupcake so it looks like they are burrowing in the grass to find the egg.

10. Store the cakes in an airtight container for up to 3 days.

CADBURY MINI EGGS ORANGE RING CAKE

The zesty flavour of this light and fluffy orange ring cake will have your taste buds tingling. Why not add some Mini Eggs magic in the middle too? This recipe is a very tasty but indulgent treat, best enjoyed on special occasions.

SERVES 16
PREP TIME 20 MINS
COOKING TIME
35–45 MINS

225g butter, softened
225g self-raising flour, plus extra for dusting
200g caster sugar
4 large free-range eggs
1 tsp baking powder
grated zest and juice of 2 oranges
30g Cadbury Mini Eggs, plus 16 extra for the centre (optional)

FOR THE ORANGE GLAZE
120g icing sugar
1–2 tbsp fresh orange juice

You will need a cake ring or bundt tin

1. Preheat the oven to 180°C/160°C fan/gas mark 4. Grease a 25cm bundt tin or cake ring with a little of the butter and dust it lightly with flour, shaking off any excess.

2. Using a food mixer or a hand-held electric whisk, beat the butter and sugar until they are light and creamy. Beat in the eggs one at a time, adding a little flour with each one to prevent it curdling.

3. Sift in the flour and baking powder and mix on a low speed until everything is well combined. Add the orange zest and juice and whisk until the mixture is smooth. If it is still a bit thick, add a splash of milk to slacken it.

4. Pour the mixture into the prepared tin and level the top. Bake in the preheated oven for 35–45 minutes until the cake is golden and well risen and a thin skewer inserted into it comes out clean. Leave the cake to cool in the tin for 15 minutes and then turn it out on to a wire rack over a large plate.

5. Put the Cadbury Mini Eggs into a sealable plastic bag and smash them into small pieces with a rolling pin or meat mallet. Alternatively, pulse them in a food processor or crush them in a pestle and mortar.

6. To make the orange glaze sift the icing sugar into a bowl and stir in the orange juice until the mixture is smooth. If the mix is too thick, thin it with more orange juice.

PER SERVING

| 263 kcals | 13.5g fat | 8g sat fat |
| 22.7g sugar | 0.2g salt |

7. Drizzle the glaze over the cake, allowing it to trickle down the sides, sprinkle the Mini Eggs on top, and leave it to set. To serve, place the cake on a pretty plate and cut it into slices. If you like, you can pile some whole Cadbury Mini Eggs in the central well and serve one with each slice. Store in an airtight container. This cake is best eaten within 3–4 days.

MINI EGGS CHOCOLATE BIRD'S NEST

These Mini Eggs chocolate bird's nests are incredibly easy to make. They're so gorgeously crunchy and chocolatey that your friends will be asking for them again and again.

MAKES 12
PREP TIME 15 MINS
COOKING TIME 5 MINS

200g Cadbury Bournville chocolate, broken into squares
25g butter
2 tbsp golden syrup
85g shredded wheat, crushed
36 Cadbury Mini Eggs

1. Line a 12-hole muffin tin with paper cases.
2. Put the chocolate, butter and golden syrup into a heatproof bowl and set it over a pan of simmering water so the base does not touch the water. Stir gently until the chocolate melts and is smooth. Alternatively, melt it in a microwave in 30-second bursts, taking out the bowl and stirring the chocolate between bursts.
3. Take the pan off the heat and stir in the shredded wheat until it's thoroughly coated.
4. Spoon the mixture into the paper cases to make little nests, and place 3 Cadbury Mini Eggs in the centre of each one.
5. Put the nests in the fridge and chill them for 1–2 hours until they are solid. Store the nests in a sealed container in the fridge for up to 4 days.

PER SERVING

178 kcals | 8.1g fat | 4.5g sat fat
17g sugar | 0.04g salt

MINI TIP

THE BIRD'S NESTS LOOK REALLY PRETTY IF YOU VARY THE COLOURS OF THE MINI EGGS IN EACH ONE.

MINI EGGS EASTER CAKE

The smooth frosting, moist sponge and crunchiness of shredded wheat and Mini Eggs is such a mouth-watering combination that your friends and family will be asking you to make this cake all year round! This recipe is a very tasty but indulgent treat, best enjoyed on special occasions. **Photograph overleaf.**

SERVES 12
PREP TIME 25 MINS
COOKING TIME 20–25 MINS
CHILLING TIME 1 HOUR

175g butter, softened
175g soft brown sugar
3 medium free-range eggs
150g self-raising flour
30g cocoa powder

PER SERVING

372 kcals	20.6g fat	10.5g sat fat
25.3g sugar		0.2g salt

1. Preheat the oven to 180°C/160°C fan/gas mark 4. Grease two 18cm sandwich tins and line them with baking parchment.
2. Using a food mixer or a hand-held electric whisk, beat the butter and sugar until light and creamy. Beat in the eggs one at a time, adding a little flour with each egg to prevent curdling. Sift in the flour and cocoa powder and mix on a low speed until everything is well combined. Add the milk and beat the mixture until it is smooth.
3. Divide the mixture between the prepared tins and level the tops. Bake the cakes in the preheated oven for 20 minutes until they are well risen and a thin skewer inserted into them comes out clean. Leave to cool in the tins.
4. To make the chocolate frosting put all the ingredients into a bowl and beat until they are smooth with a hand-held electric whisk.
5. Turn out the cakes and peel off the lining paper. Place one cake on a plate and spread half the frosting over it. Cover this with the other cake and spread the rest of the frosting over the top.

FOR THE CHOCOLATE FROSTING

80g smooth peanut butter
4 tbsp maple syrup
3 tbsp cocoa powder
2 tbsp skimmed milk
a few drops of vanilla extract

FOR THE CHOCOLATE NEST

100g Cadbury Bournville chocolate, broken into squares
50g shredded wheat
12 Cadbury Mini Eggs

6. To make the nest melt the chocolate in a heatproof bowl over a pan of simmering water. Alternatively, melt it in a bowl in a microwave in 30-second bursts, taking out the bowl and stirring the chocolate between bursts. Take the bowl off the heat and stir in the shredded wheat until it's well coated.

7. Grease a bowl with a 6cm base and line it with cling film. Put the chocolate mixture into the bowl and mould it around the base and sides, raising it above the edge of the bowl to make a nest. Chill in the fridge for an hour, or until the mixture has set hard.

8. Peel off the cling film and place the nest on top of the cake. Fill it with the Cadbury Mini Eggs and serve. You can store the cake in an airtight container for up to 3 days.

MINI EGGS FUDGE BROWNIE BITES

These succulent fudge brownie bites with the chocolatey goodness of Mini Eggs are great for little ones – and they'll melt in the mouths of adults too.

MAKES 24
PREP TIME 15 MINS
COOKING TIME 12–15 MINS

150g soft brown sugar

50ml sunflower oil

1 tsp vanilla extract

2 medium free-range eggs

85g plain flour

½ tsp baking powder

50g cocoa powder, plus extra for dusting

25g milk chocolate chips

24 Cadbury Mini Eggs

1. Preheat the oven to 180°C/160°C fan/gas mark 4. Line a 24-hole mini muffin tin with small paper cases.
2. Beat together the sugar, oil and vanilla extract in a bowl. Beat in the eggs and then sift in the flour, baking powder and cocoa powder. Stir the mixture in a figure-of-eight motion with a metal spoon until everything is smooth and well combined. Stir in the chocolate chips, distributing them evenly throughout the mixture.
3. Divide the mixture between the paper cases and gently push a Mini Egg into the centre of each one. Bake the brownie bites in the preheated oven for 12–15 minutes until they are cooked but still squidgy inside.
4. Cool the brownie bites on a wire rack and when they are cold, dust them lightly with cocoa powder. Store them in an airtight tin and eat within 4–5 days.

MINI TIP

INSTEAD OF COCOA POWDER, LIGHTLY DUST THE BROWNIE BITES WITH ICING SUGAR.

PER SERVING

67 kcals | 3.8g fat | 1.3g sat fat

9.5g sugar | 0.03g salt

MINI EGGS STRAWBERRY SURPRISE CAKE

This Mini Eggs strawberry surprise cake is unsurprisingly delicious. The fresh zing of the strawberries mixed with the lightness of the sponge makes this a dreamy fruity treat. Photograph overleaf.

SERVES 10
PREP TIME 30 MINS
COOKING TIME 20–25 MINS

5 large free-range eggs, separated
130g caster sugar, plus extra for dusting
130g plain flour
1 tsp baking powder
300g strawberries
20 Cadbury Mini Eggs

1. Preheat the oven to 180°C/160°C fan/gas mark 4. Grease two 20cm sandwich tins and line the bases with baking parchment.
2. Put the egg yolks and sugar into a bowl and beat them with a hand-held electric whisk for at least 5 minutes until you have a mixture that is thick, creamy and very pale in colour.
3. Sift the flour and baking powder into a bowl and set them aside.
4. In another bowl, whisk the egg whites until they stand in fairly stiff peaks.
5. Using a metal spoon, gently fold some egg white into the whisked egg yolk mixture, using a figure-of-eight motion. Next, fold in some of the sifted flour and baking powder. Keep alternating until both are used up, finishing with the egg white.
6. Divide the mixture between the lined tins and bake the cakes in the preheated oven for 20–25 minutes until the sponge is risen and golden. Press one lightly with your finger and if it springs back it's cooked. Leave them to cool in the tins on a rack for 10 minutes and then turn them out on to some baking parchment dusted with sugar.
7. To make the frosting beat the soft cheese until it's smooth and then beat in the yoghurt, icing sugar and vanilla extract.

PER SERVING

216 kcals | 6.2g fat | 2.8g sat fat
15g sugar | 0.3g salt

FOR THE FROSTING
180g extra-light soft cheese
100g thick 0% fat Greek yoghurt
2 tbsp icing sugar
a few drops of vanilla extract

8. Remove the lining paper from the sponges. Place one on to a serving plate, cut out the centre with a 6cm cookie cutter and spread with half the frosting. Keep 10 strawberries for decoration and cut the rest in half. Place these on top of the frosting.
9. Fill the hole with the Cadbury Mini Eggs and place the second sponge on top.
10. Cover the top of the cake with the rest of the frosting and place the rest of the strawberries around the edge. To serve, cut the cake into slices and give everyone a Mini Egg with a piece of cake. The cake will keep in an airtight container in the fridge for 24 hours.

TURN TO PAGE 52 FOR THE MINI EGGS STRAWBERRY SHORTCAKE TARTLETS

FIND MINI EGGS KRACKOLATES ON PAGE 48

SWEET TREATS, COOKIES & FUN SNACKS

MINI EGGS FROZEN BANANA LOLLIES

Your friends will go bananas for these easy-to-make frozen lollies – the perfect mixture of chocolate, banana and crunchy Mini Eggs.

MAKES 8

PREP TIME 20 MINS

FREEZING TIME 10–11 HOURS

4 small ripe bananas
60g Cadbury Mini Eggs
100g Cadbury Bournville chocolate, broken into squares
½ tsp coconut oil

You will need 8 wooden lolly sticks

1. Line a baking tray with baking parchment.
2. Peel the bananas and cut them in half horizontally (not lengthways). Insert a lolly stick into each sliced end and place the bananas side by side on the lined tray. Freeze for at least 10 hours.
3. Put the Cadbury Mini Eggs into a sealable plastic bag and smash them into small pieces with a rolling pin or meat mallet. Alternatively, crush them in a pestle and mortar. Spread the pieces out on a plate.
4. When you're ready to make the lollies, put the chocolate squares and coconut oil in a glass bowl and microwave it over a medium heat for 30 seconds. Take the bowl out and stir the mixture, then repeat until the chocolate has melted. Alternatively, place the chocolate and oil in a heatproof bowl set over a pan of gently simmering water. When the chocolate is melted and glossy, remove the pan from the heat immediately.
5. Dip a frozen banana half into the melted chocolate and then roll it in the crushed Cadbury Mini Eggs. Repeat with the remaining banana halves and replace them on the lined tray. Return them to the freezer for at least 30 minutes. They will keep in the freezer for 2–3 days.

PER SERVING

148 kcals | 5.5g fat | 3.3g sat fat
18g sugar | 0.04g salt

MINI TIP

THESE LOLLIES ARE A DELICIOUS AND EASY SNACK OR EVEN A DESSERT TO MAKE AHEAD AND KEEP IN THE FREEZER UNTIL REQUIRED.

MINI EGGS KRACKOLATES

A Mini Eggs twist on the much-loved cornflake cake brings even more crunch to these krackolates. And they're quick to make when you want a tasty treat fast.

MAKES 12
PREP TIME 15 MINS
CHILLING TIME 1 HOUR

75g butter
3 tbsp golden syrup
3 tbsp cocoa powder
3 tbsp icing sugar
grated zest of 1 orange
200g cornflakes
12 Cadbury Mini Eggs

1. Place 12 paper cases in a 12-hole muffin tin.
2. Put the butter and golden syrup in a pan and melt them over a low heat.
3. Remove the pan from the heat and stir in the cocoa powder and icing sugar.
4. Stir in the orange zest and add the cornflakes a few at a time. Fold them in gently until they are thoroughly coated.
5. Divide the mixture between the paper cases and place a Mini Egg in the centre of each one. Chill them in the fridge for at least 1 hour, or until they are set. The krackolates will keep well in the fridge for 4–5 days.

PER SERVING

158 kcals	6g fat	3g sat fat
7.3g sugar	0.09g salt	

MINI EGGS CHOCOLATE DIPPED VIENNESE FINGERS

These buttery, crumbly shortbread biscuits covered in chocolate with the added crunch of Mini Eggs will inspire you to do a Viennese waltz around the kitchen for joy.

MAKES 30

PREP TIME 25 MINS

CHILLING TIME 30 MINS

COOKING TIME 10–12 MINS

100g butter, softened
25g icing sugar
100g plain flour, sifted
½ tsp baking powder
1 tsp cornflour
1 tsp vanilla extract
60g Cadbury Mini Eggs
200g Cadbury Dairy Milk chocolate, broken into squares

You will need a piping bag with a large star-shaped nozzle

1. Line 2 baking trays with baking parchment.
2. In a food mixer or with a hand-held electric whisk, beat the butter and icing sugar until they are pale and fluffy – this will take about 5 minutes. Beat in the flour, baking powder, cornflour and vanilla extract.
3. Spoon the mixture into a piping bag with a large star-shaped nozzle and pipe 30 x 6cm fingers on to the lined baking trays, leaving some space around each one. Chill them in the fridge for 30 minutes.
4. While the fingers are chilling preheat the oven to 180°C/160°C fan/gas mark 4. Bake the fingers in the preheated oven for 10–12 minutes until they are cooked and pale golden. Transfer them to a wire rack and leave them to cool.
5. Put the Cadbury Mini Eggs into a sealable plastic bag and smash them into small pieces with a rolling pin or meat mallet. Alternatively, crush them in a pestle and mortar. Transfer the pieces to a bowl.
6. Melt the Cadbury Dairy Milk chocolate squares in a heatproof bowl over a pan of gently simmering water. Alternatively put the bowl in a microwave for 20–30-second bursts, taking the bowl out and stirring the chocolate between bursts.
7. Dip one end of each finger into the melted chocolate and place them on baking parchment. Sprinkle them with the crushed Cadbury Mini Eggs, pressing the pieces in gently. When the chocolate has set, store the fingers in an airtight container for up to 2–3 days.

PER SERVING

85 kcals	5.1g fat	1.8g sat fat
5.9g sugar	0.01g salt	

MINI EGGS STRAWBERRY SHORTCAKE TARTLETS

Crumbly, velvety shortcake mixed with the fresh sweetness of strawberries make these tartlets perfect for an after-dinner treat.

MAKES 12 TARTLETS
PREP TIME 20 MINS
CHILLING TIME 15–30 MINS
COOKING TIME 6–8 MINS

100g butter
3 tbsp caster sugar
120g plain flour, plus extra for dusting
½ tsp baking powder
a pinch of salt
12 Cadbury Mini Eggs
200g 0% fat Greek yoghurt
200g fresh strawberries

PER SERVING

| 139 kcals | 7.6g fat | 4.5g sat fat |
| 4.5g sugar | 0.06g salt |

1. Lightly butter a 12-hole tartlet tin.
2. In a food mixer or with a hand-held electric whisk, beat the butter and sugar until they are pale and creamy. Beat in the flour, baking powder and salt.
3. Roll the mixture into a ball and knead it lightly with your hands. Cover it with cling film or put it in a plastic bag and chill it in the fridge for 15–30 minutes to firm up. Preheat the oven to 170°C/150°C fan/gas mark 3.
4. On a lightly floured surface, roll out the dough until it is 5mm thick, and cut out 6cm circles with a pastry cutter or a saucer. Place the circles in the tartlet tin, press them down lightly and prick them with a fork.
5. Bake the tartlets in the oven for 6–8 minutes until they are cooked and golden brown. Remove them from the tin and cool them on a wire rack.
6. Put the Cadbury Mini Eggs into a sealable plastic bag and smash them into small pieces with a rolling pin or meat mallet. Alternatively, crush them in a pestle and mortar. Put three-quarters of the pieces into a bowl and mix in the yoghurt.
7. Keep 6 strawberries for decoration and chop the rest. Mix them into the yoghurt and divide the mixture between the tartlets. Sprinkle the remaining crushed Mini Egg pieces on top. Halve the rest of the strawberries and decorate the tartlets with them. Store in a sealed container in the fridge for up to 2 days.

MINI EGGS TRAIL MIX

This trail mix is a great lunchbox treat – and the berries, nuts and seeds are healthy for all the family. Smashed up Mini Eggs add a lovely chocolate crunch to this delicious snack.

SERVES 18
PREP TIME 10 MINS

80g Cadbury Mini Eggs

180g mixed nuts, e.g. almonds, peanuts, shelled pistachios

40g unsweetened coconut flakes

40g mixed sunflower and pumpkin seeds

50g dried cranberries

100g low-sugar granola

1. Put the Cadbury Mini Eggs into a sealable plastic bag and smash them into small pieces with a rolling pin or meat mallet. Alternatively, crush them in a pestle and mortar.
2. Put the pieces in a bowl and add the remaining ingredients. Mix everything together well.
3. Transfer the mixture to an airtight screwtop jar or container. The trail mix can be stored in a cool, dry place for up to 3 weeks.

PER SERVING

| 135 kcals | 9.9g fat | 1.9g sat fat |
| 6.7g sugar | 0.2g salt | |

MINI EGGS CHOCOLATE COCONUT TRUFFLES

A gorgeous mix of velvety smooth truffle with a crunchy Mini Eggs centre.
A delicious treat for all ages – but remember to keep some for yourself!

MAKES 16
PREP TIME 20 MINS
CHILLING TIME 1 HOUR

250g soft Medjool dates, stoned
60g shredded unsweetened coconut
60g chopped almonds
2 tbsp smooth peanut butter
2 tbsp cocoa powder, plus extra for
  dusting
1 tbsp coconut oil
a few drops of vanilla extract
16 Cadbury Mini Eggs

1. Blitz the dates in a food processor until you have a sticky paste. Add two-thirds of the coconut plus the almonds, peanut butter, cocoa powder, coconut oil and vanilla extract. Blitz until the mixture is well combined. If it seems dry, add 1–2 tablespoons of water to moisten it.
2. Take a little of the mixture and use your fingers to mould it around a Mini Egg, completely covering the egg. Repeat with the remaining mixture and eggs.
3. Put the rest of the coconut on a plate and press it lightly into the truffles to cover them.
4. Place the truffles on a baking tray lined with baking parchment and chill them in the fridge for 1 hour. You can store them in an airtight container in the fridge for up to a week.

PER SERVING

132 kcals	7.2g fat	4.2g sat fat
11.1g sugar	0.05g salt	

MINI EGGS SWIRLED CHOCOLATE BARK

This bark mixes the intense flavour of dark chocolate with sweet white chocolate and zingy raspberry, then adds Mini Eggs to create a delectable delight.

MAKES 30 PIECES
PREP TIME 20 MINS
CHILLING TIME 45 MINS

120g Cadbury Mini Eggs
250g Cadbury Bournville chocolate, broken into squares
250g Cadbury White Chocolate Buttons
2 tsp freeze-dried raspberry pieces

PER SERVING

| 96 kcals | 5g fat | 3g sat fat |
| 7.7g sugar | 0.04g salt | |

1. Line a large baking tray with baking parchment.
2. Put the Cadbury Mini Eggs into a sealable plastic bag and smash them into small pieces with a rolling pin or meat mallet. Alternatively, crush them in a pestle and mortar.
3. Melt the Cadbury Bournville chocolate in a heatproof bowl over a pan of gently simmering water. Alternatively melt it in a bowl in a microwave, heating it for 20–30 seconds at a time, then taking out the bowl and stirring the chocolate between bursts.
4. Melt the Cadbury White Chocolate Buttons in a separate bowl in the same way.
5. Thinly spread the melted Bournville chocolate over the lined baking tray to make a large rectangle. Place spoonfuls of the melted white chocolate on top and swirl the chocolate with a toothpick to create a marbled effect.
6. Scatter the crushed Mini Egg pieces over the top, pressing them in lightly, and then sprinkle over the freeze-dried raspberries.
7. Chill the bark in the fridge for 45 minutes until the chocolate is set hard.
8. Cut or break the bark into 30 pieces and store it in an airtight container in the fridge to keep as solid as possible for up to 2 weeks.

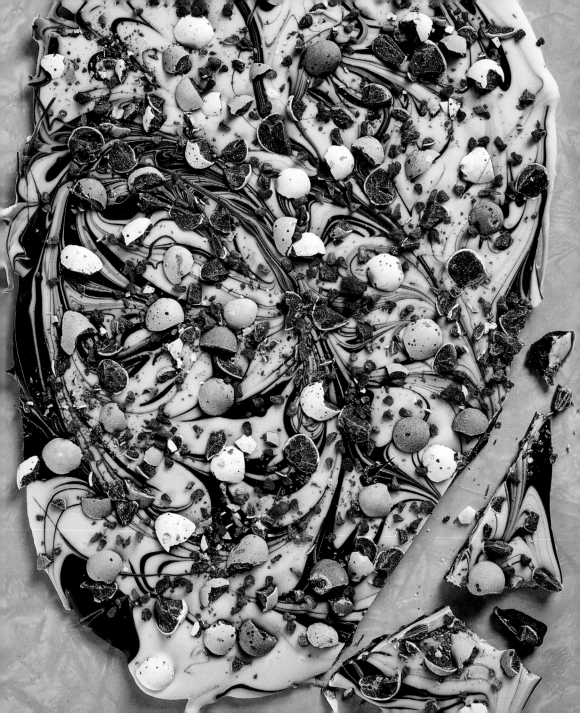

MINI EGGS
MILKSHAKE

Why not try this delicious Mini Eggs flavoured milkshake for your weekend refreshment? This recipe is a very tasty but indulgent treat, best enjoyed on special occasions.

SERVES 4
PREP TIME 10 MINS

180g Cadbury Mini Eggs
300ml chilled semi-skimmed milk
4 scoops of chocolate ice-cream
4 tbsp whipped cream
4 tsp chocolate syrup

1. Set aside 8 Cadbury Mini Eggs and put the rest in a blender with half the milk. Pulse until the Cadbury Mini Eggs have broken down into tiny pieces.
2. Add the remaining milk and the ice-cream and blend until the mixture is thick and creamy.
3. Pour the milk shake into 4 tall glasses and top each with a spoonful of whipped cream. Drizzle with the chocolate syrup and decorate with the remaining Cadbury Mini Eggs. Enjoy immediately.

MINI TIP

IF YOU DON'T HAVE SEMI-SKIMMED MILK, DON'T WORRY. USE SKIMMED, FULL-FAT OR EVEN NON-DAIRY ALMOND MILK.

PER SERVING

398 kcals	15.5g fat	12g sat fat
44g sugar	0.3g salt	

MINI EGGS FROZEN YOGHURT POPS

These frozen yoghurt pops are delightfully easy to make. A quick blitz with the blender will soon give you a creamy frozen treat to enjoy.

MAKES 10
PREP TIME 10 MINS
FREEZING TIME 6 HOURS

60g Cadbury Mini Eggs
250g blueberries
2 tbsp runny honey
500g 0% fat Greek yoghurt

You will need 10 lolly moulds

PER SERVING

| 86 kcals | 1.4g fat | 0.8g sat fat |
| 11.5g sugar | 0.07g salt | |

1. Put the Cadbury Mini Eggs into a sealable plastic bag and smash them into small pieces with a rolling pin or meat mallet. Alternatively, crush them in a pestle and mortar.
2. Blitz the blueberries in a blender until you have a thick, smooth purée. Transfer this to a bowl and stir in the honey.
3. Add the Greek yoghurt and gently swirl everything together with the crushed Cadbury Mini Eggs until the mixture is marbled cream and blue.
4. Divide the mixture between the ice lolly moulds and freeze them for 2 hours. Remove the moulds and insert a wooden stick into the centre of each one. Return the ice lollies to the moulds and freeze them for at least 4 hours until they are frozen solid.
5. To turn out the frozen yoghurt pops, run the moulds under hot water for a few seconds – don't let water get inside the moulds. The pops will keep in the freezer for up to a month.

MINI EGGS FRUITY FROZEN YOGHURT BARK

This frozen berry treat is fun to make and bursting with fruity flavour.
It combines the delicious crispiness of Mini Eggs with zingy berries to make
a crunchy bark that keeps well in the freezer.

SERVES 12
PREP TIME 15 MINS
FREEZING TIME 6 HOURS

250g strawberries
60g Cadbury Mini Eggs
500g 0% fat Greek yoghurt
2 tbsp runny honey
75g berries, e.g. whole raspberries
or chopped strawberries

PER SERVING

| 66 kcals | 1g fat | 0.6g sat fat |
| 9g sugar | 0.08g salt | |

1. Line a 20 x 30cm baking tray with cling film, smoothing it out flat and letting it hang over the edges of the tray.
2. Blitz the strawberries to a purée in a food processor or blender.
3. Put the Cadbury Mini Eggs into a sealable plastic bag and smash them into small pieces with a rolling pin or meat mallet. Alternatively, crush them in a pestle and mortar.
4. Mix together the yoghurt and honey in a bowl and then gently spread it over the lined baking tray, pushing it into the corners.
5. Drop teaspoonfuls of the strawberry purée over the top and swirl them into the yoghurt with a toothpick to create a marbled effect. Sprinkle with the smashed Cadbury Mini Eggs and dot with the berries, pressing them in lightly.
6. Freeze for 6 hours, or until the bark is frozen solid. Remove the tray from the freezer, peel away the cling film and break the bark into 12 pieces. This keeps well in the freezer in bags or an airtight container for up to 2 months.

MINI EGGS DIP

A new fondue for Mini Eggs fans! Choose your dippers – this recipe goes with anything from fruit to breadsticks. Best served at a party and enjoyed while deliciously velvety and warm.

SERVES 10
PREP TIME 10 MINS

160g Cadbury Mini Eggs
4 tbsp double cream

FOR THE DIPPERS
Breadsticks
Pretzel sticks
Biscotti
Whole strawberries with stems
Thickly-sliced bananas
Satsuma or orange segments
Fresh pineapple chunks
Seedless grapes
Pitted cherries
Melon chunks
Mango or papaya chunks

1. Put the Cadbury Mini Eggs into a sealable plastic bag and smash them into medium to small pieces with a rolling pin or meat mallet. Alternatively, crush them in a pestle and mortar.
2. Place the crushed Cadbury Mini Eggs in a heatproof bowl set over a pan of simmering water. Stir gently until the chocolate melts.
3. Remove the pan from the heat and stir in the cream, so you have a glossy mixture with small chunks of candy.
4. Transfer the mixture to a serving bowl and set it in the middle of a large serving plate or dish containing the dippers. Let people help themselves to the Mini Egg dip while it's still warm.

PER SERVING

106 kcals	6.4g fat	3g sat fat
10.8g sugar	0.03g salt	

62

MINI EGGS CHOCOLATE CHIP COOKIES

These chocolate chip cookies melt in your mouth and the Mini Eggs add a lovely crunch. Keep them in a cookie jar – they're not likely to last long! Photograph overleaf.

MAKES 14
PREP TIME 20 MINS
COOKING TIME 10–12 MINS

80g Cadbury Mini Eggs
125g butter, at room temperature
125g soft light brown sugar
1 large free-range egg, beaten
a few drops of vanilla extract
250g plain flour
½ tsp bicarbonate of soda
100g Cadbury Dairy Milk chocolate, chopped into small pieces

MINI TIP
YOU CAN USE CHOPPED DARK CADBURY BOURNVILLE CHOCOLATE OR WHITE CHOCOLATE INSTEAD OF CADBURY DAIRY MILK.

1. Preheat the oven to 180°C/160°C fan/gas mark 4. Line a large baking tray with baking parchment.
2. Put aside 14 Cadbury Mini Eggs and place the rest in a sealable plastic bag. Smash them into small pieces with a rolling pin or meat mallet. Alternatively, crush them in a pestle and mortar.
3. Beat the butter and sugar together in a food mixer or with a hand-held electric whisk until light and fluffy. Gradually beat in the egg, a little at a time, and then add the vanilla extract, flour, bicarbonate of soda, chopped Cadbury Dairy Milk chocolate and half the crushed Cadbury Mini Eggs. Mix on a low speed to the consistency of a soft dough.
4. Divide the dough into 14 pieces and roll each one into a ball. Arrange the balls on the lined baking tray, spacing them out well, and press down lightly to flatten them. Divide the remaining Cadbury Mini Eggs between them, pushing them into the dough.
5. Bake in the preheated oven for about 10–12 minutes until they are cooked and golden. Cool them on a wire rack and store them in an airtight container for up to 5 days.

PER SERVING

245 kcals	12g fat	4g sat fat
16.5g sugar	0.1g salt	

CINNAMON OAT AND MINI EGGS COOKIES

Golden and crumbly cookies that combine the mouth-watering flavour of cinnamon with delicious oats. Enjoy them warm from the oven while the chocolate is still gooey.

MAKES 12
PREP TIME 15 MINS
CHILLING TIME 15 MINS
COOKING TIME 12–15 MINS

125g butter, softened
125g soft brown sugar
1 large free-range egg, beaten
½ tsp vanilla extract
125g rolled oats
100g plain flour
½ tsp bicarbonate of soda
¼ tsp salt
1 tsp ground cinnamon
80g Cadbury Mini Eggs

PER SERVING

203 kcals	13g fat	3.3g sat fat
14.5g sugar	0.1g salt	

1. Line a large baking sheet with baking parchment.
2. Beat the butter and sugar together in a food mixer or with a hand-held electric whisk until light and fluffy. Gradually beat in the egg a little at a time, then add the vanilla extract.
3. Add the rolled oats, flour, bicarbonate of soda, salt and cinnamon. Mix on a low speed to the consistency of a soft dough.
4. Put 12 Cadbury Mini Eggs aside and place the rest in a sealable plastic bag. Smash them into largish pieces with a rolling pin or meat mallet. Alternatively, crush them in a pestle and mortar. Mix them into the dough, distributing them evenly throughout. Chill the dough in the fridge for 15 minutes to firm up. Preheat the oven to 180°C/160°C fan/gas mark 4.
5. Divide the dough into 12 pieces and roll each piece into a ball. Arrange them on the lined baking tray, spacing them out well, and press down lightly to flatten them a little. Divide the remaining Cadbury Mini Eggs between them, pushing them into the dough.
6. Bake the cookies in the preheated oven for 12–15 minutes until they are golden. Cool them on a wire rack and store them in an airtight container for up to 5 days.

MINI EGGS CHOCOLATE GRANOLA TRUFFLES

These luxurious truffles combine velvety rich dark chocolate with sweet coconut and crunchy granola to create delectable bite-sized treats.

MAKES 30
PREP TIME 15 MINS
CHILLING TIME 2 HOURS

200g Cadbury Bournville chocolate, broken into squares
1 tbsp coconut oil
1 tbsp maple syrup
150g plain low-sugar granola
30 Cadbury Mini Eggs

You will need 30 extra-small paper or foil cases

1. Put 30 truffle cases (extra-small foil or paper cases) on a baking tray.
2. Melt the Cadbury Bournville chocolate, the coconut oil and the maple syrup in a heatproof bowl over a pan of gently simmering water. Or put the bowl in a microwave for 20–30 seconds at a time, taking out the bowl and stirring the mixture between bursts.
3. Remove the bowl from the heat and stir in the granola. If the clusters are very large, break them up into smaller pieces. Make sure the granola is well coated with melted chocolate.
4. Divide the mixture between the truffle cases and place a Mini Egg in the centre of each one.
5. Chill in the fridge for 2 hours until the truffles have set solid. Store them in an airtight container in the fridge. They will keep well for up to 5 days.

PER SERVING (TRUFFLE)

77 kcals | 3.9g fat | 2g sat fat
6.5g sugar | 0.03g salt

MINI EGGS COCONUT BIRDS' NESTS

Crunchy, chocolatey snacks that combine the sweetness of coconut with sticky peanut butter. This recipe is a very tasty but indulgent treat, best enjoyed on special occasions.

MAKES 24
PREP TIME 15 MINS
COOKING TIME 6–8 MINS
CHILLING TIME 2 HOURS

sunflower oil, for brushing

150g unsweetened shredded coconut

300g Cadbury Dairy Milk chocolate, broken into squares

1 tbsp smooth peanut butter

160g Cadbury Mini Eggs

1. Preheat the oven to 200°C/180°C fan/gas mark 6. Lightly brush the wells of a 24-hole mini muffin tin with oil and set it aside. If you use a silicone pan you won't need to do this.

2. Spread out the coconut on a baking tray and toast it in the preheated oven for 6–8 minutes until it is pale golden brown. Check it regularly to make sure it does not burn. Remove the tray from the oven and set it aside to cool.

3. Melt the chocolate in a heatproof bowl over a pan of gently simmering water. Or you can put the bowl in a microwave for 20–30 seconds at a time, taking out the bowl and stirrring the chocolate between bursts.

4. Stir in the peanut butter until the mixture is smooth. Add the toasted coconut and stir well until it is coated.

5. Drop spoonfuls of the mixture into the mini muffin tin and mould each one into a nest shape. Fill the nests with the Cadbury Mini Eggs.

6. Chill the nests in the fridge for at least 2 hours until they are set solid. You can store them in the fridge in an airtight container for up to 5 days.

PER SERVING

148 kcals	9.5g fat	6.9g sat fat
12g sugar	0.02g salt	

SUPER SPEEDY EASTER FUDGE NIBBLES

Easter fudge nibbles that are so easy to make you'll probably be making them all year round. A treat for adults and kids alike.

MAKES 36
PREP TIME 20 MINS
CHILLING TIME 2–3 HOURS

160g Cadbury Mini Eggs
150g Cadbury Bournville chocolate
150g Cadbury Dairy Milk chocolate, broken into squares
100ml condensed milk
1 tsp vanilla extract
a pinch of sea salt flakes

1. Line a 20 x 20cm cake tin with baking parchment.
2. Put the Cadbury Mini Eggs into a sealable plastic bag. Smash them into small pieces with a rolling pin or meat mallet. Alternatively, crush them in a pestle and mortar.
3. Put the chocolate and condensed milk in a heatproof bowl and set it over a pan of gently simmering water. Stir occasionally until the chocolate melts and you have a smooth mixture.
4. Take the bowl off the heat and stir in the vanilla extract and sea salt. Add two-thirds of the crushed Cadbury Mini Eggs and mix gently to distribute them through the mixture.
5. Pour the mixture into the lined tin and level the top. Sprinkle it with the remaining Mini Egg pieces and push them in lightly.
6. Chill the fudge in the fridge for 2–3 hours until it is set and solid. Remove and cut the fudge into 36 squares. Store it in an airtight container in the fridge for up to 1 week.

PER SERVING

| 74 kcals | 3.5g fat | 2.1g sat fat |
| 9.2g sugar | 0.03g salt | |

FIND FRUITY SMOOTHIE BOWLS ON PAGE 76

GO TO PAGE 86
FOR CHOCOLATE WAFFLES

BRUNCHES &
BREAKFASTS

MINI EGGS FRUITY YOGHURT SMOOTHIE BOWL

This smoothie recipe has the perfect breakfast mix of fruit and fibre – and then adds Mini Eggs for a chocolate treat.

SERVES 6
PREP TIME 10 MINS

600g frozen mixed berries,
   e.g. blueberries, raspberries,
   strawberries, blackberries
4 bananas, frozen and sliced
480ml unsweetened almond milk
6 tbsp 0% fat Greek yoghurt
30g Cadbury Mini Eggs

FOR THE TOPPING
12 Cadbury Mini Eggs
2 tbsp desiccated or shaved coconut
100g fresh berries

1. Blitz the frozen berries, bananas, almond milk, yoghurt and Cadbury Mini Eggs in a blender or food processor until you have a smooth purée flecked with tiny pieces of Mini Egg.
2. Divide the smoothie mixture between 6 serving bowls and top with the whole Cadbury Mini Eggs, coconut and berries. Eat immediately while the smoothie is still slightly frozen.

PER SERVING

| 199 kcals | 5g fat | 2.8g sat fat |
| 19.8g sugar | 0.1g salt | |

MINI EGGS RASPBERRY & ALMOND OVERNIGHT OATS

Something yummy for breakfast that combines almond milk with oats and tops them with zingy raspberries. This recipe makes Mini Eggs the best sort of eggs to eat in the morning.

SERVES 4
PREP TIME 15 MINS
CHILLING TIME
OVERNIGHT

500g 0% fat Greek yoghurt

120ml unsweetened almond or soya milk

12 tbsp rolled or porridge oats

2 tbsp mixed seeds, e.g. chia, flax, sunflower

1 tbsp maple syrup or runny honey

2–3 drops of vanilla extract

30g Cadbury Mini Eggs

200g raspberries

1 banana, sliced

2 tbsp toasted flaked almonds

1. Put the yoghurt, milk, oats, seeds, maple syrup or honey and vanilla extract into a bowl and mix well.
2. Divide the mixture between 4 serving bowls, then cover and leave them in the fridge overnight.
3. Put the Cadbury Mini Eggs into a sealable plastic bag and smash them into small pieces with a rolling pin or meat mallet. Alternatively, crush them in a pestle and mortar.
4. The following morning, cover the oat mixture with the raspberries and sliced banana, and sprinkle with the crushed Cadbury Mini Eggs and flaked almonds just before serving.

PER SERVING

250 kcals	7.6g fat	2.2g sat fat
19.5g sugar	0.2g salt	

YOGHURT, BERRY & GRANOLA LAYERED POTS WITH MINI EGGS TOPPING

A great breakfast bite or lunchbox snack, these easy-to-make Mini Eggs pots contain creamy yoghurt, sweet berries and crunchy granola to make a tasty morning treat. Photograph overleaf.

SERVES 6
PREP TIME 15 MINS

60g Cadbury Mini Eggs
500g 0% fat Greek yoghurt
1 tsp vanilla extract
300g mixed berries, e.g. strawberries, raspberries, blueberries
6 tsp runny honey
120g plain low-sugar granola

You will need 6 small pots, jars or tumblers

1. Put the Cadbury Mini Eggs into a sealable plastic bag and smash them into small pieces with a rolling pin or meat mallet. Alternatively, crush them in a pestle and mortar.
2. Mix the yoghurt and vanilla extract in a bowl. Spoon half the yoghurt into 6 small glass pots, jars or tumblers.
3. Top the yoghurt with most of the berries and cover them with the remaining yoghurt. Drizzle the top with the honey.
4. Mix the granola and crushed Cadbury Mini Eggs together and sprinkle them over the top. Top with the remaining fruit and enjoy!

MINI TIP

IF YOU'RE IN A HURRY, YOU CAN ASSEMBLE THE LAYERED YOGHURT, BERRIES AND HONEY IN JARS THE NIGHT BEFORE. CHILL THEM IN THE FRIDGE OVERNIGHT AND SPRINKLE THEM WITH THE CRUSHED CADBURY MINI EGGS, GRANOLA AND REMAINING BERRIES THE FOLLOWING MORNING. SCREW ON THE LIDS AND HAVE BREAKFAST ON THE GO!

PER SERVING

215 kcals	6.2g fat	1.7g sat fat
15g sugar	0.2g salt	

MINI EGGS CHOCOLATE BREAKFAST PANCAKES

Whip up some chocolate breakfast pancakes for breakfast. Velvety pancakes that ooze deliciously melted chocolate all over the plate will set you up for the day!

MAKES 14
PREP 15 MINS
COOKING TIME 10–15 MINS

100g Cadbury Mini Eggs
2 large free-range eggs
220ml semi-skimmed milk
5 tbsp vegetable oil, plus extra for cooking
160g plain flour
2 tsp baking powder
30g cocoa powder
½ tsp salt
1 tbsp caster sugar
Greek yoghurt and fresh raspberries or strawberries, to serve (optional)

1. Put the Cadbury Mini Eggs into a sealable plastic bag and smash them into small pieces with a rolling pin or meat mallet. Alternatively, crush them in a pestle and mortar.

2. In a bowl, beat together the eggs, milk and vegetable oil until they are well blended.

3. Sift the flour, baking powder and cocoa powder into a large bowl and stir in the salt and sugar. Make a well in the centre and pour in the beaten egg mixture. Stir gently until everything is well combined. Gently stir in the crushed Cadbury Mini Eggs, being careful not to overmix.

4. Set a large frying pan over a medium to high heat and lightly brush it with oil. When it's really hot, drop 3 or 4 tablespoons of batter into the pan, leaving plenty of space between them. When bubbles appear on the surface after 1–2 minutes, flip the pancakes over and cook them for 1–2 minutes more until they are set and browned underneath. Remove the pancakes and keep them warm on a wire rack set over a baking tray in a medium oven, or covered loosely with foil while you make the rest of the pancakes.

5. Serve the pancakes piping hot, with some Greek yoghurt and fresh berries, if using.

**PER SERVING
(PANCAKE WITHOUT
YOGHURT AND BERRIES)**

149 kcals	7.5g fat	2.1g sat fat
6.4g sugar	0.07g salt	

82

MINI EGGS BANANA OAT MUFFINS

These healthy Mini Eggs muffins are a gorgeously gooey banana-flavoured treat.
They'll be so popular you'll have no choice but to serve them in bunches.

MAKES 12
PREP TIME 15 MINS
COOKING TIME 20 MINS

80g Cadbury Mini Eggs
100g rolled oats
200g plain flour
2 tsp baking powder
½ tsp bicarbonate of soda
a pinch of ground cinnamon
¼ tsp salt
100g soft light brown sugar
2 large ripe bananas
2 large free-range eggs, beaten
60g butter, melted

1. Preheat the oven to 180°C/160°C fan/gas mark 4. Line a 12-hole muffin tin with paper cases.
2. Put the Cadbury Mini Eggs into a sealable plastic bag and smash them into small pieces with a rolling pin or meat mallet. Alternatively, crush them in a pestle and mortar.
3. Mix together the oats, flour, baking powder, bicarbonate of soda, cinnamon, salt and sugar in a large bowl. Make a well in the centre.
4. In another bowl coarsely mash the bananas with a fork and mix the beaten egg and melted butter into them. Add this mixture to the dry oat mixture, then fold it through gently with a metal spoon until everything is just combined. Finally, stir in the smashed Cadbury Mini Eggs. Do not overmix. Divide the mixture between the paper cases.
5. Bake the muffins in the preheated oven for about 20 minutes until they are slightly risen and golden brown. You can test whether they are cooked by inserting a skewer into the middle of one – it should come out clean.
6. Cool the muffins on a wire rack before serving them warm or cold. You can store them in an airtight container for 2–3 days.

PER SERVING

231 kcals	8.3g fat	2.3g sat fat
12.5g sugar		0.1g salt

MINI EGGS CHOCOLATE WAFFLES

These chocolatey waffles are a delicious way to start the morning. Pile them up and tuck into a perfect mix of gooey melted chocolate and crunchy Mini Eggs.

MAKES 6
PREP TIME 15 MINS
COOK TIME 15–20 MINS (DEPENDING ON WAFFLE IRON)

150g plain flour
2 tsp baking powder
½ tsp salt
1 tsp ground cinnamon
50g caster sugar
3 tbsp cocoa powder
240ml unsweetened almond milk
2 medium free-range eggs, beaten
1 tsp vanilla extract
3 tbsp melted butter
spray oil to cook the waffles

FOR THE TOPPING
30g Cadbury Mini Eggs
8 tbsp dairy-free coconut yoghurt

You will need a waffle iron

1. Sift the flour, baking powder and salt into a large bowl and stir in the cinnamon, sugar and cocoa powder.
2. Make a well in the centre and stir in the milk, beaten eggs, vanilla extract and melted butter. Mix until you have a thick, smooth batter.
3. Preheat a waffle iron and lightly spray it with oil – if you have a non-stick waffle iron there's no need to do this. Ladle in some of the batter, then seal the iron and follow the manufacturer's instructions until the waffle is cooked. Keep it warm on a wire rack set over a baking tray in a medium oven, or covered loosely with foil while you cook the remaining waffles in the same way.
4. Meanwhile, put the Cadbury Mini Eggs into a sealable plastic bag and smash them into medium to large pieces with a rolling pin or meat mallet. Alternatively, crush them in a pestle and mortar.
5. Serve the hot waffles topped with the coconut yoghurt and crushed Cadbury Mini Eggs.

PER SERVING (PANCAKE WITHOUT YOGHURT AND BERRIES)

275 kcals | 12.5g fat | 6.7g sat fat
11.3g sugar | 0.2g salt

BLUEBERRY, YOGHURT AND MINI EGGS CRUNCH

Smooth fruity yoghurt combines perfectly with crunchy Mini Eggs and granola in a tasty breakfast pot. These take just **10** minutes to prepare, but we guarantee they'll be gone in half that time.

SERVES 4
PREP TIME 10 MINS

60g Cadbury Mini Eggs
250g 0% fat Greek yoghurt
200g blueberries
8 tbsp low-sugar granola
4 tsp mixed seeds, e.g. pumpkin,
    sunflower, sesame

1. Put the Cadbury Mini Eggs into a sealable plastic bag and smash them into small pieces with a rolling pin or meat mallet. Alternatively, crush them in a pestle and mortar.
2. Spoon half the yoghurt into the bottom of 4 tall glasses or small glass bowls.
3. Place most of the blueberries on top of the yoghurt and then sprinkle them with the granola and half the crushed Cadbury Mini Eggs.
4. Cover this layer with the remaining yoghurt, smoothing the top, and sprinkle it with the seeds and the rest of the crushed Cadbury Mini Eggs. Top with the rest of the blueberries and eat the granola immediately while the yoghurt is chilled and the topping is really crunchy.

PER SERVING

243 kcals | 5.7g fat | 3.4g sat fat
18g sugar | 0.1g salt

88

MINI EGGS LATTE

A creamy Mini Eggs latte offers you a luxurious treat to start your day and will give you just the kick you need to get going in the morning.

SERVES 4
PREP TIME 15 MINS

60g Cadbury Mini Eggs
4 shots hot espresso (or 4 pods)
4 tsp chocolate sauce
400ml semi-skimmed milk
8 tbsp aerosol whipped cream

1. Put the Cadbury Mini Eggs into a sealable plastic bag and smash them into medium to large pieces with a rolling pin or meat mallet. Alternatively, crush them in a pestle and mortar.
2. Pour the espresso into 4 cups or small mugs and stir a teaspoon of chocolate sauce into each cup.
3. Heat and froth the milk with the steamer attachment of an espresso machine. Alternatively, heat the milk in a pan and froth it with a hand-held electric frother.
4. Pour the frothed milk slowly and steadily into the cups from quite high above. The milk should pour into the cups first with the froth following as you lower the jug towards the cup.
5. Top the cups with the whipped cream and crushed Cadbury Mini Eggs. Enjoy!

MINI TIP
FULL-FAT MILK ALSO FROTHS REALLY WELL.

PER SERVING

158 kcals	6.4g fat	3.9g sat fat
18g sugar	0.1g salt	

SEE MERINGUE CADBURY
MINI EGG AND FLAKE NESTS
ON PAGE 116

FIND SPEEDY MINI EGGS
BRÛLÉE ON PAGE 109

DESSERTS

MINI EGGS EASTER PAVLOVA

This Easter-themed dessert takes a while to cook, but is worth the wait. Adding crunchy Mini Eggs and velvety Dairy Milk chocolate to the mix results in a very tasty but indulgent treat, best enjoyed on special occasions.

SERVES 10
PREP TIME 25 MINS
COOKING TIME 1¼ –1½ HOURS

4 large free-range egg whites
200g caster sugar
1 tsp white wine vinegar
2 tsp cornflour
1 tsp vanilla extract
300ml whipping cream
1 tbsp icing sugar
100g Cadbury Dairy Milk chocolate, broken into squares
30 Cadbury Mini Eggs

PER SERVING

298 kcals	16g fat	10.2g sat fat
32g sugar	0.1g salt	

1. Preheat the oven to 140°C/120°C fan/gas mark 1. Line a large baking sheet with non-stick baking parchment and draw a 23cm diameter circle on it.

2. Whisk the egg whites in a clean dry bowl until they form stiff peaks. Gradually beat in the sugar a little at a time, until the meringue is stiff and glossy. Whisk in the vinegar, cornflour and vanilla extract.

3. Spoon the meringue on to the circle you have drawn on the baking parchment, swirling it out to the edges and making a slight indent in the middle.

4. Cook the meringue in the preheated oven for 1¼–1½ hours, then turn off the oven, leaving the meringue inside until it is completely cold.

5. Gently remove the baking parchment from the meringue base and place the base on a serving plate.

6. Whip the cream and icing sugar until it stands in stiff peaks, then spread it over the meringue.

7. Melt the chocolate in a bowl in the microwave in 30-second bursts, taking out the bowl and stirring the chocolate between bursts. Alternatively, melt it in a bowl set over a pan of gently simmering water.

8. Drizzle the melted chocolate in a zigzag pattern over the top of the pavlova. Decorate the pavlova with the Cadbury Mini Eggs and cut it into slices to serve.

MINI EGGS CHOCOLATE ESPRESSO MOUSSE

This light, bubbly, creamy espresso mousse is a perfect pick-me-up. It's easy to make and will soon become a favourite treat after dinner.

SERVES 6

PREP TIME 20 MINS

CHILLING TIME 3–4 HOURS

100g Cadbury Bournville chocolate, broken into squares

2 tbsp strong espresso coffee (1 shot)

1 medium free-range egg, separated, plus 2 egg whites

2 tsp caster sugar

50g 0% fat Greek yoghurt

30g Cadbury Mini Eggs

1. Put the chocolate in a bowl in a microwave and melt it in 30-second bursts, taking out the bowl and stirring the chocolate between bursts. Alternatively, place it in a bowl set over a pan of gently simmering water. Stir in the espresso coffee and remove the bowl from the heat.
2. Beat the egg whites in a clean dry bowl until they stand in stiff peaks. Beat in the sugar.
3. In another bowl beat the egg yolk and stir it into the melted chocolate with the yoghurt.
4. Gently fold in the egg whites in a figure-of-eight movement with a metal spoon, and divide the mousse between 6 ramekins or glass dishes. Chill them in the fridge for 3–4 hours until they are set.
5. Put the Cadbury Mini Eggs into a sealable plastic bag and smash them into medium to large pieces with a rolling pin or meat mallet. Sprinkle the pieces over the mousses and serve.

PER SERVING

135 kcals	6.4g fat	3g sat fat
13.8g sugar	0.01g salt	

95

MINI EGGS CREAMY SUMMER FRUIT MERINGUE CRUSH

This summer snack is bursting with berries and zesty lemon flavour combined with crunchy meringue and Mini Eggs – it's tantalisingly good.

SERVES 6
PREP TIME 15 MINS

60g Cadbury Mini Eggs
2 tbsp lemon curd
500g 0% fat Greek yoghurt
6 large meringue shells, roughly
  crumbled
300g mixed raspberries and
  strawberries
2 ripe peaches, stoned and diced
grated zest of 1 lemon

1. Put the Cadbury Mini Eggs into a sealable plastic bag and smash into medium to large pieces with a rolling pin or meat mallet.
2. Swirl the lemon curd into the yoghurt. Spoon one-third of the yoghurt into 6 tall glasses or glass sundae dishes.
3. Sprinkle half the meringue fragments into each glass on top of the yoghurt, then top them with crushed Cadbury Mini Eggs, berries and peaches.
4. Cover this with half the remaining yoghurt and add the rest of the meringue fragments, Cadbury Mini Eggs and fruit, keeping a few berries and some chocolate pieces for decoration.
5. Cover the fruit with the rest of the yoghurt and sprinkle the top with the lemon zest. Decorate the top with the rest of the berries and the last pieces of crushed Cadbury Mini Eggs. Serve immediately or cover the dishes with cling film and chill them in the fridge until required.

PER SERVING

160 kcals	2.7g fat	1.6g sat fat
20g sugar	0.2g salt	

QUICK MINI EGGS CHOCO MOCHA AFFOGATO

Pressed for time? This quick coffee-inspired recipe is a delicious blend of hot mocha chocolate and cold ice-cream – perfect for cooling down on a warm summer's day.

SERVES 4
PREP TIME 15 MINS

240ml freshly made, piping hot, strong espresso coffee (4 long shots)
200g good-quality vanilla ice-cream
60g Cadbury Mini Eggs

PER SERVING

167 kcals	6.3g fat	3g sat fat
20g sugar		0.1g salt

1. Chill 4 small glasses or coffee cups.
2. Put the Cadbury Mini Eggs into a sealable plastic bag and smash them into medium to large pieces with a rolling pin or meat mallet.
3. Mix most of the crushed Cadbury Mini Eggs into the vanilla ice-cream, keeping a few for later.
4. Use a 50g ice-cream scoop to put a scoop of ice-cream into each chilled glass or cup. Pour over the hot espresso and sprinkle the top with the remaining crushed Mini Egg pieces.
5. Serve immediately while the ice-cream is still cold and starting to melt and the espresso is hot.

MINI EGGS RASPBERRY CHOUX RING

Light and airy yet crispy and fruity, this twist on a popular pudding will put your pastry skills to the test and result in a delicious treat at the end.

SERVES 8
PREP TIME 30 MINS
COOLING TIME 10 MINS
COOKING TIME 30–35 MINS

50g butter
150ml water
75g plain flour, sifted
a pinch of salt
2 large free-range eggs, beaten
60g Cadbury Mini Eggs
500g 0% fat Greek yoghurt
½ tsp vanilla extract
25g icing sugar
200g whole raspberries

You will need a piping bag with a rose nozzle

PER SERVING

| 191 kcals | 8.3g fat | 4.6g sat fat |
| 11.6g sugar | 0.2g salt | |

1. Preheat the oven to 200°C/180°C fan/gas mark 6. Line a baking tray with baking parchment and place a 20cm diameter plate on top. Draw round it with a pencil.
2. Put the butter and water in a saucepan and set it over a low to medium heat. When the butter melts, turn up the heat and bring the mixture to the boil.
3. Remove the pan from the heat immediately and tip in the flour and salt. Beat the mixture well with a wooden spoon until you have a smooth ball that leaves the sides of the pan clean.
4. Set the pan aside to cool for 10 minutes and then beat in the egg a little at a time. When it is all added and you have a glossy mixture, spoon or pipe it in a circle on the baking parchment using a piping bag with a large rose nozzle.
5. Bake the choux ring in the preheated oven for 30–35 minutes until it is well risen and golden brown. Slice the ring in half horizontally and cool it on a wire rack.
6. Put the Cadbury Mini Eggs into a sealable plastic bag and smash them into medium pieces with a rolling pin or meat mallet.
7. Mix the yoghurt with the vanilla extract and 2 tablespoons of the icing sugar. Stir in the crushed Cadbury Mini Eggs.
8. Fill the choux ring with the yoghurt mixture and raspberries. Lightly dust it with the remaining icing sugar and serve cut into slices.

MINI EGGS DRIZZLED FROZEN YOGHURT STRAWBERRIES

These frozen strawberry bites are so simple to make. They combine the bitterness of melted chocolate with smashed Mini Eggs for a sweet treat that leaves a lovely zing in the mouth.

SERVES 6
PREP TIME 20 MINS
FREEZING TIME 1–2 HOURS

400g strawberries, ideally with stalks and leaves attached
250g 0% fat Greek yoghurt
60g Cadbury Mini Eggs
100g Cadbury Bournville chocolate, broken into squares

PER SERVING

176 kcals | 6.7g fat | 4g sat fat

19g sugar | 0.2g salt

1. Hold each strawberry by its leaves, lifting them up and away from the fruit, and dip it into a shallow bowl of Greek yoghurt. Leave a little bit of red berry showing below the leaves at the top.
2. Place the dipped strawberries – leaf-side down and tip up – on a wire rack that fits in the freezer. Alternatively, arrange them on a baking tray lined with baking parchment or waxed paper.
3. Freeze the strawberries for at least 1 hour, or until the yoghurt is set and frozen. If you have any yoghurt left over, you can dip the frozen strawberries again to give them a second coat and return them to the freezer for another hour.
4. Put the Cadbury Mini Eggs into a sealable plastic bag and smash them into small to medium pieces with a rolling pin or meat mallet.
5. Put the chocolate into a bowl and put it into a microwave for 30-second bursts, taking out the bowl and stirring the chocolate between bursts. Alternatively place it in a bowl set over a pan of gently simmering water.
6. Remove the frozen strawberries from the freezer and drizzle the melted chocolate over the top. Sprinkle them with the crushed Cadbury Mini Eggs, pressing them lightly into the chocolate.
7. Return the strawberries to the freezer for 20–30 minutes until the chocolate is set. Serve as a dessert or a snack.

MINI TIP

INSTEAD OF DRIZZLING WITH MELTED CHOCOLATE AND CRUSHED CADBURY MINI EGGS, DRIZZLE THE FROZEN STRAWBERRIES WITH CADBURY MINI EGGS SAUCE INSTEAD (SEE PROFITEROLES RECIPE ON PAGE 114) THEN POP THEM BACK INTO THE FREEZER UNTIL THEY ARE FROZEN SOLID.

FROZEN BERRIES WITH WHITE CHOCOLATE MINI EGGS SAUCE

Covered in creamy melted white chocolate and crushed Mini Eggs, these yummy frozen berries are ripe for the picking.

SERVES 6
PREP TIME 10 MINS
FREEZING TIME 20–30 MINS

600g mixed berries, e.g. raspberries, blueberries, blackberries, strawberries
60g Cadbury Mini Eggs
100g Cadbury White Chocolate Buttons, broken into pieces
4 tbsp single cream

1. Spread out the berries on a large plate or a baking tray. Place the tray in the freezer for 20–30 minutes until the berries are slightly frozen but not solid.
2. Put the Cadbury Mini Eggs into a sealable plastic bag and smash them into small to medium pieces with a rolling pin or meat mallet.
3. Just before serving, put the White Chocolate Buttons in a bowl in a microwave and melt them in 30-second bursts, taking out the bowl and stirring the chocolate between bursts. Alternatively, melt it in a bowl set over a pan of gently simmering water.
4. Add half the crushed Cadbury Mini Eggs and stir so the pieces start to melt into the chocolate. Stir in the cream.
5. Divide the frozen berries between 6 bowls and drizzle the creamy white chocolate sauce over the top. Sprinkle with the rest of the crushed Cadbury Mini Eggs and serve immediately.

MINI TIP

ANY FROZEN BERRIES WORK WELL. MOST SUPERMARKETS STOCK HANDY PACKS OF MIXED BERRIES IN THEIR FREEZER AISLES.

PER SERVING

170 kcals	8g fat 4.5g	sat fat 20g
sugar 0.12g		salt

MINI EGGS CHOCOLATE MINT RAMEKINS

Taste the mint in these Mini Eggs chocolate ramekins. They're a treat for any dinner party – or to keep in the fridge for when you need to satisfy a sweet craving.

SERVES 6
PREP TIME 15 MINS
COOKING TIME 5–10 MINS
CHILLING TIME 30 MINS

100g Cadbury Bournville chocolate, broken into squares

1 tbsp cocoa powder

3 tbsp hot water

2 medium free-range eggs, separated

1 tsp butter

1 tbsp caster sugar

a few drops of natural peppermint extract

12 Cadbury Mini Eggs

PER SERVING

151 kcals	8.3g fat	4.2g sat fat
15g sugar	0.05g salt	

1. Melt the chocolate in a heatproof bowl set over a pan of gently simmering water.
2. Blend the cocoa powder with the hot water and then stir it into the melted chocolate until it is smooth. Set the bowl aside to cool slightly, but don't let it go cold.
3. Beat the egg yolks in another bowl and then stir them into the chocolate. Replace the bowl over the pan of simmering water and stir gently for at least 5 minutes until the mixture thickens. Add the butter, sugar and peppermint extract to taste. Stir well and remove the bowl from the heat.
4. In a clean dry bowl, whisk the egg whites until they are firm and stay on the whisk when you lift it out of the bowl. Fold them gently into the chocolate mixture with a metal spoon in a figure-of-eight movement until everything is thoroughly mixed.
5. Divide half the mixture between 6 small ramekins. Place a Mini Egg on top of each and then cover them with the remaining chocolate mixture. Chill the ramekins in the fridge for at least 30 minutes.
6. Meanwhile crush the remaining Cadbury Mini Eggs by putting them in a sealable plastic bag and smashing them into small to medium pieces with a rolling pin or meat mallet. Serve the ramekins chilled and sprinkled with the crushed Cadbury Mini Eggs.

MINI EGGS FRUITY FILO PARCELS

Who doesn't love a parcel – especially one filled with Mini Eggs and fruity goodness? These filo parcels are a delicious combination of crisp pastry with soft peach inside and will tickle your taste buds!

SERVES 4
PREP TIME 10 MINS
COOKING TIME 10–15 MINS

4 x 15g sheets filo pastry
1 medium free-range egg, beaten
30g Cadbury Mini Eggs
4 amaretti biscuits, crushed
4 tbsp 0% fat Greek yoghurt
2 ripe peaches, halved, peeled and stoned
1 tbsp icing sugar

1. Preheat the oven to 200°C/180°C fan/gas mark 6. Line a baking tray with baking parchment.
2. Lightly brush each sheet of filo pastry with beaten egg. Fold them in half sideways and brush them with more beaten egg.
3. Crush the Cadbury Mini Eggs by putting them in a sealable plastic bag and smashing them into small to medium pieces with a rolling pin or meat mallet.
4. In a bowl, mix together the crushed Cadbury Mini Eggs, amaretti biscuit pieces and yoghurt. Divide the mixture between the peach halves, filling the hollow and piling the rest on top.
5. Place a filled peach half in the middle of each filo pastry sheet and bring up the corners to meet at the top in the centre. Pinch the edges together at the top with your fingers to seal them. Brush the parcels with the rest of the beaten egg and place them on the lined baking tray.
6. Bake the parcels in the preheated oven for 10–15 minutes until they are crisp and golden brown. Serve immediately dusted with icing sugar.

PER SERVING

165 kcals	3.5g fat	1.3g sat fat
15g sugar	0.03g salt	

MINI EGGS
BAKED ALASKAS

A retro classic with a Mini Eggs twist. You'll love the indulgent mixture of crunchy meringue, sweet vanilla ice-cream and fresh raspberries. This recipe is a very tasty but indulgent treat, best enjoyed on special occasions.

SERVES 4
PREP TIME 15 MINS
FREEZING TIME 1–2 HOURS

COOKING TIME 3–4 MINS

30g Cadbury Mini Eggs
4 x 2cm-thick slices of chocolate Swiss roll
4 x 50ml scoops of good-quality vanilla ice-cream
2 medium free-range egg whites
75g caster sugar
fresh raspberries, to serve (optional)

You will need 4 individual ovenproof dishes about 20 x 15 x 4cm

1. Crush the Cadbury Mini Eggs by putting them into a sealable plastic bag and smashing them into small pieces with a rolling pin or meat mallet.
2. Place the Swiss roll slices in 4 individual ovenproof dishes and put a scoop of ice-cream on top of each one. Pop them into the freezer for 1–2 hours until the ice-cream is frozen solid.
3. Preheat the oven to 220°C/200°C fan/gas mark 7.
4. In a clean dry bowl, whisk the egg whites until they are stiff. Gradually whisk in the sugar a little at a time, until the meringue is really glossy.
5. Take the dishes of frozen Swiss roll and ice-cream out of the freezer. Sprinkle the crushed Cadbury Mini Eggs over the top of the ice-cream and the visible cake edges. Place them on a baking tray.
6. Spoon the meringue evenly over the top and sides of the dishes to completely enclose the ice-cream and cake.
7. Bake in the preheated oven for 3–4 minutes until the meringue is golden brown. Eat immediately with some fresh raspberries, if you like.

PER SERVING

337 kcals	10.8g fat	5.5g sat fat
20g sugar		0.2g salt

SPEEDY MINI EGGS BRÛLÉE

A twist on classic crème brûlée, these are ridiculously quick and easy to make. Break through the crackle of the caramel to find the crunchy Mini Eggs below.

SERVES 6
PREP TIME 15 MINS
COOKING TIME 4–5 MINS

60g Cadbury Mini Eggs
600g 0% fat Greek yoghurt
a few drops of vanilla extract
150g ripe apricots, stoned and diced
3 tbsp demerara sugar

1. Put the Cadbury Mini Eggs into a sealable plastic bag and smash them into small pieces with a rolling pin or meat mallet. Alternatively, use a pestle and mortar to crush them.
2. Put the yoghurt in a bowl and stir in the vanilla extract, diced apricots and crushed Cadbury Mini Eggs.
3. Divide the mixture between 6 heatproof ramekin dishes and smooth the tops. Sprinkle the sugar over the top to lightly cover the yoghurt.
4. Preheat the grill to high. When it's really hot, place the ramekins on a baking tray underneath and grill them for 4–5 minutes until the sugar melts and caramelizes. Keep checking them to make sure the sugar doesn't burn.
5. Remove the ramekins immediately and leave them to cool. Eat the brûlée lukewarm or chill it in the fridge before serving.

PER SERVING

140 kcals | 2.2g fat | 1.4g sat fat
18g sugar | 0.1g salt

CHOCOLATE ORANGE MINI EGGS WHIP

A must for chocolate orange fans, the zest in these creamy orange whips tingles on the tongue. And they're quick to whip up for pudding.

SERVES 4
PREP TIME 20 MINS
CHILLING TIME 30 MINS

30g Cadbury Mini Eggs
50g Cadbury Bournville chocolate, broken into squares
1 tbsp cocoa powder
2 tbsp hot water
250g extra-light soft cheese
grated zest and juice of 1 orange
2 medium free-range egg whites
1 tbsp caster sugar
orange segments, to decorate (optional)

1. Put the Cadbury Mini Eggs into a sealable plastic bag and smash them into small pieces with a rolling pin or meat mallet. Alternatively, use a pestle and mortar to crush them.
2. Melt the Cadbury Bournville chocolate in a heatproof bowl set over a pan of gently simmering water. Blend the cocoa powder with the hot water and then stir it into the melted chocolate until it is smooth. Set the bowl aside to cool a little.
3. Put the soft cheese into a bowl with the orange zest and juice and mix well. Beat in the melted chocolate mixture. Stir in most of the crushed Cadbury Mini Eggs, keeping some for decoration.
4. In a clean dry bowl, whisk the egg whites until they are stiff and glossy. Beat in the sugar. Using a figure-of-eight motion, stir the beaten egg whites into the soft cheese mixture with a metal spoon.
5. Spoon the mixture into 4 glass sundae dishes or tall glasses and chill them in the fridge for at least 30 minutes.
6. Before serving, sprinkle the tops with the rest of the crushed Mini Egg pieces and decorate them with orange segments, if using.

PER SERVING

198 kcals	8.8g fat	4.3g sat fat
20g sugar	0.3g salt	

EASY FRUITY MINI EGGS ICE-CREAM

This homemade ice-cream is packed with fruity flavour and Mini Eggs crunch. And the inside scoop? This delicious pudding only takes 20 minutes to prepare. This recipe is a very tasty but indulgent treat, best enjoyed on special occasions.

SERVES 8
PREP TIME 20 MINS
FREEZING TIME 4–5 HOURS

250g mixed berries, e.g. raspberries, blueberries, chopped strawberries
80g Cadbury Mini Eggs
300ml double cream
250ml condensed milk
a few drops of vanilla extract

You will need a 500g loaf tin

1. Line a 500g loaf tin with a double layer of cling film to make unmoulding the ice-cream easier.
2. Put all the berries into a bowl and crush them by pressing down with a fork until a lot of the juice runs out.
3. Put the Cadbury Mini Eggs into a sealable plastic bag and smash them into medium and small pieces with a rolling pin or meat mallet.
4. Using a food mixer or a hand-held electric whisk, beat the cream until it forms stiff peaks. Add the condensed milk and vanilla extract, and beat everything together briefly so it is combined.
5. Fold in the crushed berries and Cadbury Mini Eggs, distributing them evenly through the ice-cream mixture and swirling in the fruit juice.
6. Pour the mixture into the lined loaf tin and wrap the tin in cling film. Cover it with kitchen foil and freeze it for at least 4–5 hours or overnight.
7. To serve the ice-cream, you can either remove it from the tin and slice it like a terrine, or scoop it out.

PER SERVING

332 kcals	23g fat	14.5g sat fat
26.4g sugar	0.1g salt	

MINI TIP

YOU CAN ALSO SERVE THIS WITH CADBURY MINI EGGS SAUCE (SEE PROFITEROLES RECIPES ON PAGE 114).

113

MINI EGGS PROFITEROLES

Wow your guests with profiteroles boasting Mini Eggs both inside and out! These gorgeous pastries ooze with cream and are drizzled in chocolate sauce. It doesn't get much better. This recipe is a very tasty but indulgent treat, best enjoyed on special occasion.

SERVES 8
PREP TIME 35 MINS
COOKING TIME 20–25 MINS

50g butter
150ml water
75g plain flour, sifted
a pinch of salt
2 large free-range eggs, beaten
60g Cadbury Mini Eggs
150ml whipping cream

PER SERVING

271 kcals	19g fat	11.6g sat fat
12.3g sugar	0.12g salt	

1. Preheat the oven to 200°C/180°C fan/gas mark 6. Line 2 baking trays with baking parchment.
2. Put the butter and water in a saucepan and set it over a low to medium heat. When the butter melts, turn up the heat and bring the mixture to the boil.
3. Remove the pan from the heat immediately and tip in the flour and salt. Beat well with a wooden spoon until you have a smooth ball of mixture that leaves the sides of the pan clean.
4. Set the mixture aside to cool for 10 minutes and then beat in the egg a little at a time. When it is all added and you have a glossy mixture, spoon or pipe it using a piping bag with a 1cm plain nozzle into small mounds (a little bigger than a walnut) on to the lined baking trays. Make sure you leave plenty of room between the profiteroles as they will expand as they cook.
5. Bake the profiteroles in the preheated oven for 20–25 minutes, or until they are well risen and golden brown. Place them on a wire rack, make a hole in each one with a sharp knife and leave them to cool.
6. Put the Cadbury Mini Eggs into a sealable plastic bag and smash them into small pieces with a rolling pin or meat mallet.

FOR THE SAUCE

80g Cadbury Mini Eggs
2 tbsp double cream

You will need a piping bag with a
   1cm plain nozzle

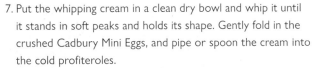

7. Put the whipping cream in a clean dry bowl and whip it until
   it stands in soft peaks and holds its shape. Gently fold in the
   crushed Cadbury Mini Eggs, and pipe or spoon the cream into
   the cold profiteroles.
8. To make the sauce, crush the Cadbury Mini Eggs into small pieces
   in a pestle and mortar and place them in a heatproof bowl set
   over a pan of simmering water. Stir gently until the chocolate
   melts, then remove the pan from the heat and stir in the cream
   so you have a glossy sauce.
9. Divide the profiteroles between 8 dishes and drizzle the warm
   sauce over the top. Serve immediately. Alternatively, pile the
   profiteroles in a mound on a serving plate and drizzle them with
   the sauce then ask people to help themselves.

MERINGUE MINI EGGS AND FLAKE NESTS

Crunchy meringue nests topped with flaky chocolate and creamy fat-free yoghurt combine to make a yummy pudding that will melt in your mouth.

MAKES 12
PREP TIME 20 MINS
COOKING TIME 2 HOURS

3 medium free-range egg whites
150g caster sugar
200g fat-free fromage frais or 0% fat Greek yoghurt
1 Cadbury Flake
24 Cadbury Mini Eggs

You will need a piping bag with a large star nozzle

1. Preheat the oven to 110°C/90°C fan/gas mark ¼. Line 2 baking trays with baking parchment.
2. In a clean dry bowl, beat the egg whites until they stand in stiff peaks. Beat in the sugar a little at a time until the whites are really glossy.
3. Spoon the mixture into a piping bag fitted with a large star nozzle and pipe 12 x 5cm circles of meringue on to the lined baking trays. Leave a hollow in the centre of each one.
4. Bake the meringues in the preheated oven for 2 hours, or until they are crisp. Leave them to cool and then peel off the baking parchment.
5. Fill the cold meringues with the fromage frais or yoghurt and crumble the Cadbury Flake over the top so they look like little nests. Fill them with the Cadbury Mini Eggs and serve.

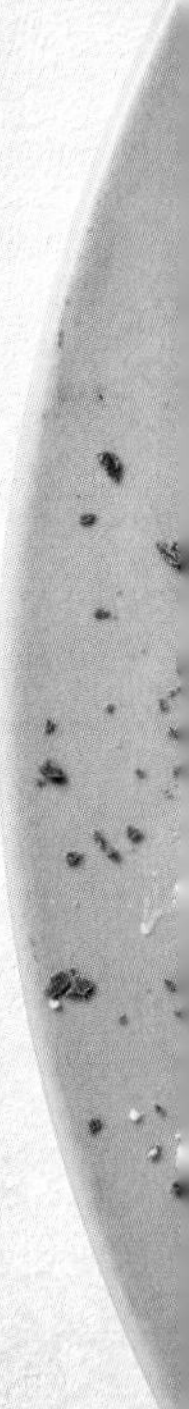

PER SERVING

104 kcals | 1.4g fat | 1.1g sat fat
15g sugar | 0.02g salt

MINI EGGS VANILLA CHEESECAKE

Everyone loves cheesecake and this one is especially smooth and creamy, with a crumbly biscuit base. The crunch from the Mini Eggs really is the icing on this delicious and indulgent cheesecake. This recipe is a very tasty but indulgent treat, best enjoyed on special occasions.

SERVES 10
PREP TIME 25 MINS
CHILLING TIME
OVERNIGHT

FOR THE GINGERNUT BASE
100g gingernut biscuits
25g butter, melted

FOR THE FILLING
300g light soft cheese
150g 0% fat Greek yoghurt
50g caster sugar
1 tsp vanilla extract
100ml double cream
1 sachet powdered gelatine
4 tbsp hot water
80g Cadbury Mini Eggs

PER SERVING

204 kcals	9g fat	6.6g sat fat
	14.8g sugar	0.4g salt

1. Line the base of a 20cm loose-bottomed or springform tin with baking parchment.
2. To make the base crush the gingernuts with a rolling pin and stir in the melted butter. Press the mixture into the base of the lined tin and level the top. Chill the base in the fridge while you make the filling.
3. In a bowl, beat the soft cheese with the yoghurt, sugar and vanilla extract.
4. In a clean dry bowl, beat the cream with a hand-held electric whisk until it stands in stiff peaks.
5. Put the hot water into a small bowl, sprinkle the gelatine over it and stir well. Leave it for 2–3 minutes, stirring occasionally, until the gelatine is completely dissolved and clear. Stir it into the soft cheese mixture and then gently fold in the whipped cream.
6. Put the Cadbury Mini Eggs into a sealable plastic bag and smash them into medium and small pieces with a rolling pin or meat mallet.
7. Arrange most of the crushed Cadbury Mini Eggs over the biscuit base and pour the cheesecake mixture over the top. Chill the cheesecake in the fridge overnight until it is set. Sprinkle it with the remaining crushed Cadbury Mini Eggs and serve it cut into slices.

MINI EGGS
NO-COOK
CHOCOLATE TARTLETS

No need to turn on the oven to make these mouth-watering, bite-sized tartlets. With smooth chocolate and sweet vanilla, this recipe is perfect when you want to make a speedy treat.

MAKES 18
PREP TIME 15 MINS
CHILLING TIME 1 HOUR

90ml semi-skimmed milk

1 tbsp caster sugar

2 tbsp butter

150g Cadbury Bournville chocolate, broken into squares

½ tsp vanilla extract

18 mini cooked shortcrust pastry tartlet cases

18 Cadbury Mini Eggs

1. Put the milk, sugar and butter into a saucepan and set over a high heat, stirring until the sugar dissolves, the butter melts and the milk starts to boil.

2. Reduce the heat and stir in the chocolate and vanilla extract. When the chocolate has melted and the mixture is smooth, remove the pan from the heat and cool the mixture slightly.

3. Spoon the chocolate mixture into the tartlet cases and decorate each one with a Mini Egg. Place the cases on a baking tray and chill them in the fridge for 1 hour until they are set. You can store the tartlets in an airtight container in the fridge for 3–4 days.

PER SERVING

| 105 kcals | 5.7g fat | 3g sat fat |
| 8.5g sugar | 0.04g salt |

MINI EGGS BANOFFEE DESSERT

This dessert is one for banoffee pie fans – a twist on a classic that's delectably sticky and sweet.

SERVES 4
PREP TIME 15 MINS
COOKING TIME 5 MINS

4 tsp muscovado sugar
4 tsp custard powder
300ml skimmed milk
60g Cadbury Mini Eggs
2 medium free-range egg whites
300g 0% fat Greek yoghurt
2 medium bananas, thinly sliced
cocoa powder for dusting

1. In a large bowl, blend the sugar and custard powder with 2 tablespoons of the milk until you have a smooth mixture.
2. Heat the remaining milk in a non-stick saucepan until it is almost boiling, then stir it into the custard mixture. Return the custard to the pan and stir it over a medium heat until it thickens. You should end up with smooth toffee-coloured custard. Transfer it to a bowl, cover it with cling film and set it aside to cool.
3. Put the Cadbury Mini Eggs into a sealable plastic bag and smash them into small to medium pieces with a rolling pin or meat mallet.
4. In a clean, dry bowl, whisk the egg whites until stiff. Stir the yoghurt into the cold custard, and then gently fold in the whisked egg whites in a figure-of-eight movement.
5. Divide half the custard between 4 dessert bowls and cover them with a layer of sliced banana.
6. Stir most of the crushed Cadbury Mini Eggs into the remaining custard and spoon this over the banana. Dust the tops with cocoa powder and sprinkle over the rest of the crushed Cadbury Mini Eggs. Serve immediately.

PER SERVING

220 kcals | 3.5g fat | 2g sat fat
20g sugar | 0.05g salt

MINI EGGS TIRAMISU

Who doesn't love a 'pick-me-up' dessert? This tiramisu is rich and creamy, and it boasts the scrummy addition of Mini Eggs. The perfect dinner party pud.

SERVES 6
PREP TIME 20 MINS

125ml very hot, strong black coffee, e.g. espresso
12 sponge fingers
2 free-range egg yolks
2 tbsp caster sugar
200g light soft cheese
150g 0% fat Greek yoghurt
2–3 drops of vanilla extract
30g Cadbury Mini Eggs
4 tsp cocoa powder

PER SERVING

| 167 kcals | 6.4g fat | 3g sat fat |
| 14g sugar | 0.3g salt | |

1. Pour the hot coffee into a wide bowl and dip 3 of the sponge fingers briefly into the coffee. Divide them between 6 small glass dishes or wine glasses. Be quick or they will start to fall apart.
2. Beat the egg yolks and sugar with a wooden spoon or electric whisk until they are really pale, thick and creamy. Beat in the soft cheese, yoghurt and vanilla extract.
3. Put the Cadbury Mini Eggs into a sealable plastic bag and smash them into small pieces with a rolling pin or meat mallet. Alternatively, crush them in a pestle and mortar.
4. Gently fold three-quarters of the Mini Egg pieces into the soft cheese mixture. Cover the coffee-soaked sponge fingers with half the mixture.
5. Dip the remaining sponge fingers into what's left of the coffee and layer them on top of the soft cheese mixture.
6. Cover the sponge fingers with the remaining soft cheese, smoothing the top, and dusting it lightly with cocoa powder. Sprinkle with the remaining Mini Egg pieces.
7. Chill the tiramisu in the fridge for at least 1 hour to firm up before serving.

MINI TIP

YOU CAN SUBSTITUTE TRIFLE SPONGES FOR THE SPONGE FINGERS.

INDEX